Contents

Preface

The *Śrī Upadeśāmṛta* is highly revered in the Śrī Gauḍīya Vaiṣṇava spiritual community (*sampradāya*). Resplendent with the inner sentiments (*bhāva*) and outer complexion of Śrīmatī Rādhikā, Śrī Caitanya Mahāprabhu is the inaugurator of the congregational chanting of Śrī Kṛṣṇa's holy names (*śrī-nāma-saṅkīrtana*) and the bestower of that most elevated, radiant divine love for Śrī Kṛṣṇa which had never been given before. For the benefit of all living beings, Śrīla Rūpa Gosvāmī churned the ocean of Śrīman Mahāprabhu's instructions and extracted the essence in the form of the *Śrī Upadeśāmṛta*. The instructions given in this book are indispensable for practitioners (*sādhakas*) of the devotional path (*bhakti*). Without following these instructions, entering the realm of pure devotion and especially following the intricate and elevated path of spontaneous devotion (*rāgānugā-bhakti*) is not only difficult, but impossible.

We learn from the diary of Govinda dāsa, the personal servant of the *prema-avatāra* (incarnation of divine love), Śrī Caitanya Mahāprabhu, that prior to returning to His eternal, unmanifest pastimes, Mahāprabhu remained constantly overwhelmed in a highly inflamed (*sudīpta*) mood of divine separation (*vipralambha*). At that time Mahāprabhu's two intimate, eternal servitors, Śrī Svarūpa Dāmodara and Śrī Rāya Rāmānanda, would try to pacify Him by singing verses which were relevant to His mood. On one occasion Mahāprabhu was sitting with His devotees on the shore of the ocean engaged in hearing narrations concerning Kṛṣṇa (*kṛṣṇa-kathā*). Seeing the dense grove of trees lining the shore of the blue ocean and the tall sand dunes, remembrance of Govardhana Hill and the Yamunā River with the many beautiful gardens and groves (*kuñjas*) situated on her banks suddenly sprang up inside Him. Then He began bitterly weeping in separation from Kṛṣṇa. When after sometime His excitement subsided and He became peaceful, He gave the assembled devotees some instructions in a soft and sweet voice. Those instructions comprise the verses of this *Śrī Upadeśāmṛta*.

From the very beginning it is compulsory for *sādhakas* desirous of entering the realm of *bhakti* to renounce activities which are unfavourable for progress in spiritual life. These include the urges of mind, speech, anger, tongue, stomach and genitals, as well as avoiding overeating, unnecessary endeavours, useless conversation, improper compliance with the rules and regulations of devotion, bad association, and greed or the restlessness of the mind to adopt worthless opinions. Simultaneously it is imperative to adopt those things which nourish one's *bhakti*, such as enthusiasm, determination, patience, the good behaviour associated with *bhakti* and the ideals for devotional life which have been established by pure devotees.

After progressing somewhat, one should engage in the six kinds of devotee association, give appropriate respect to the three levels of Vaiṣṇavas and serve them accordingly. Finally, while residing either physically or mentally in Vraja and following in the footsteps of devotees who possess deep love for Kṛṣṇa and who are adept at relishing the devotional mellows of Vraja (*vraja-rasa*), one should constantly engage his tongue and mind in chanting and remembering Śrī Kṛṣṇa's names (*nāma*), form (*rūpa*), qualities (*guṇa*) and pastimes (*līlā*). Just as Śrīmatī Rādhikā is the most dear to Kṛṣṇa, similarly Her pond (*kuṇḍa*) is also the most dear to Him. Therefore, practitioners of *bhakti* must certainly take shelter of the embodiment of the ultimate devotional ecstacy (*mahābhāva*), Śrīmatī Rādhikā, and Her pond, Śrī Rādhā-kuṇḍa. Śrī Caitanya Mahāprabhu completely preserved this topmost essence of all instructions within the verses of *Śrī Upadeśāmṛta.*

The Eminently Glorious Author of Śrī Upadeśāmṛta, Śrī Rūpa Gosvāmī

Who doesn't know the author of *Śrī Upadeśāmṛta*, Śrī Rūpa Gosvāmī? His ancestry was a royal dynasty of *bhāradvāja-gotrī brāhmaṇas* from Karnataka, South India, who were particularly knowledgeable in the *Yajur Veda*. Impelled by some special circumstances, his great-grandfather Śrī Padmanābha left his ancestral home and settled in Bengal in a village named Naihāṭī which is situated on the banks of the Bhāgīrathī River. Padmanābha's grandson Śrī Kumāradeva had three sons: Amara, Santoṣa and Vallabha. Later they became famous as Śrī Sanātana Gosvāmī, Śrī Rūpa Gosvāmī and Śrī Anupama. Impressed with their extraordinary scholarship, qualifications and virtuous conduct, the Muslim ruler of Bengal at that time, Hussain Shah, gave Rūpa and Sanātana the titles Sakara Mallika and Dabira Mallika and made them his prime minister and personal secretary. But after some time they came into contact with the saviour of Kali-yuga, Śrī Caitanya Mahāprabhu. Renouncing their colossal wealth and all worldly relationships, they became distinguished ascetics, fully dedicating themselves to serving the internal desire of Śrī Rādhā-Kṛṣṇa. On the order of Mahāprabhu they restored the forgotten holy places of Vraja-maṇḍala, re-established the proper methods for Deity worship, composed authoritative scriptures on *bhakti* and established the codes of good conduct for devotional life.

Again manifesting the famous Śrī Govindajī Deity in Vṛndāvana, constructing a massive and beautiful temple and establishing an opulent standard of worship for the Deity is all accredited to Śrī Rūpa Gosvāmī alone. He appeared in the year 1489 and disappeared in 1564. In Śrī Jīva Gosvāmī's *Laghu-vaiṣṇava-toṣaṇī* commentary on *Śrīmad-Bhāgavatam*, we find the following authoritative list of the literatures he composed: (1) *Śrī Haṁsadūta*, (2) *Śrī Uddhava Sandeśa*, (3) *Śrī Kṛṣṇa-janma-tithi-vidhi*, (4) *Śrī Bṛhad-kṛṣṇa-gaṇoddeśa-dīpikā*, (5) *Śrī Laghu-kṛṣṇa-gaṇoddeśa-dīpikā*, (6) *Śrī Stava-mālā*, (7) *Śrī Vidagdha-mādhava-nāṭaka*, (8) *Śrī Lalita-mādhava-nāṭaka*, (9) *Śrī Dāna-keli-kaumudī*,

(10) *Śrī Bhakti-rasāmṛta-sindhu*, (11) *Śrī Ujjvala-nīla-maṇi*, (12) *Śrī Prayuktākhya-candrikā*, (13) *Śrī Mathurā-māhātmya*, (14) *Śrī Padyāvalī*, (15) *Śrī Nāṭaka-candrikā*, (16) *Śrī Laghu-bhāgavatāmṛta*, (17) *Śrī Sāmānya-virudāvalī-lakṣaṇa* and (18) *Śrī Upadeśāmṛta*.

Śrī Rādhā-ramaṇa dāsa Gosvāmī, Author of the Upadeśa-prakāśikā Commentary

Śrī Rādhā-ramaṇa dāsa Gosvāmī composed a Sanskrit commentary on *Śrī Upadeśāmṛta*, named *Upadeśa-prakāśikā*, which is brief, yet essential. He appeared in the dynasty of the Vṛndāvana *gosvāmīs* who serve the Rādhā-ramaṇa Deity, who was established and served by Śrī Gopāla-bhaṭṭa Gosvāmī. His father's name was Śrī Govardhana-lāla Gosvāmī and his grandfather's name was Śrī Jīvana-lāla Gosvāmī. Śrī Jīvana-lāla Gosvāmī was his initiating spiritual master (*dīkṣā-guru*) and also his instructing spiritual master (*śikṣā-guru*). Rādhā-ramaṇa dāsa Gosvāmī was a great scholar, author and poet in Sanskrit and Hindi. His *Dīpikā-dīpanī* commentary on *Śrīmad-Bhāgavatam* is highly respected amongst scholars. Similarly, his *Upadeśa-prakāśikā* commentary is highly revered in Vaiṣṇava society.

Śrī Saccidānanda Bhaktivinoda Ṭhākura, Author of the Pīyūṣa-varṣiṇī-vṛtti Commentary

By composing hundreds of books on *bhakti*, Bhaktivinoda Ṭhākura re-established in this modern era, which is degraded by excessive sensual pleasure, the flow of pure devotion (*śuddha-bhakti*) which had temporarily stopped. He is an intimate, eternal devotee of Śrī Caitanya Mahāprabhu. Due to his having propagated in different ways the pure philosophy of divine love (*prema-dharma*) exhibited and preached by Śrīman Mahāprabhu, he is famous as the Seventh Gosvāmī. Because he manifested Mahāprabhu's holy names (*śrī-gaura-nāma*), Mahāprabhu's holy land (*śrī-gaura-dhāma*), Mahāprabhu's innermost desire (*śrī-gaura-kāma*) and the narrations of Mahāprabhu's pastimes (*śrī-gaura-līlā*), he is considered the incarnation of Vyāsa in Mahāprabhu's pastimes.

He appeared in an educated and cultured family on September 2, 1838, in the village of Vīranagara, which is near the place of Mahāprabhu's appearance, Śrī Dhāma Māyāpura, in West Bengal. His childhood name was Śrī Kedaranātha Datta. He was a scholarly and ingenious student. During his household life, he held a high position as a government official under the rule of the British Rāja. During that time he served the innermost desire of Śrī Gaurasundara by translating the *Upaniṣads*, the *Brahma-sūtra*, *Śrīmad-Bhāgavatam*, *Bhagavad-gītā*, the commentaries of the Gosvāmīs, composing his own devotional books, and by publishing weekly and monthly spiritual journals. In addition, he established *nāma-haṭṭa* programmes for the distribution of *hari-nāma-saṅkīrtana* and *hari-kathā* from village to village and town to town, and he revived many forgotten holy places.

In the end he renounced his wealth and family and took up permanent residence at Śrī Svānanda-sukhada-kuñja, a garden in Śrī Godruma which is situated on the banks of the divine Bhāgīrathī River within the boundary of Śrī Dhāma Navadvīpa. There he remained possessionless and established the ideal of the system for practicing spontaneous devotional worship (*rāgānugā-bhajana*). If he had not appeared in this world, Mahāprabhu's birthplace, the places where Mahāprabhu performed pastimes and Mahāprabhu's instructions would still be concealed. Today, in all corners of the world, *hari-nāma-saṅkīrtana* is being joyously celebrated and the very high waves of *śrī-gaura-kṛṣṇa bhakti* are inundating the entire world. Thousands of educated Western youths are drinking the mellows of devotion (*bhakti-rasa*) and dancing, being overcome with spiritual joy. It is none other than Bhaktivinoda Ṭhākura who again inaugurated this flow of *bhakti*.

He composed approximately one hundred books in Sanskrit, Bengali, Hindi, English, Oriya and other languages. The names of a few of them are as follows: commentaries on ancient scriptures such as *Brahma-sūtra*, *Bhagavad-gītā*, some of the Upaniṣads, *Śrīmad-Bhāgavatam*, *Śrī Caitanya-caritāmṛta*; and his own compositions such as *Jaiva-dharma*, *Śrī Caitanya-śikṣāmṛta*, *Śrī Caitanya Mahāprabhura Śikṣā*, *Datta-kaustubha*, *Śrī Kṛṣṇa-saṁhitā*, *Tattva-viveka*, *Bhajana-rahasya*, *Daśa-mūla-śikṣā*, *Śaraṇāgati*, *Gītāmālā*, *Kalyāṇa-kalpataru*, *Harināma-cintāmaṇi*, *Prema-pradīpa*, and *Śrī Caitanya Mahāprabhu–His Life and Precepts*. He disappeared from this world on June 23, 1914.

Śrī Bhaktisiddhānta Sarasvatī Gosvāmī 'Prabhupāda', Author of the Anuvṛtti Commentary

Śrī Śrīmad Bhaktisiddhānta Sarasvatī Gosvāmī 'Prabhupāda' appeared in Jagannātha Purī on Friday, February 3, 1874, the day of *kṛṣṇa-pañcamī* in the month of Māgha. His father and *śikṣā-guru* was the famous eternal devotee of Śrīman Mahāprabhu, Śrī Bhaktivinoda Ṭhākura. His childhood name was Śrī Vimalā Prasāda. From childhood he was an extraordinary scholar, a spiritual genius and righteous in his conduct. At the age of fifteen, due to his expertise in all branches of knowledge, the community of elevated Vaiṣṇavas of that time adorned him with the title 'Śrī Siddhānta Sarasvatī', which means he who personifies the wisdom of all established truths.

In 1918, he accepted the renounced order (*sannyāsa*) and became known as *parivrājakācārya* Śrī Bhaktisiddhānta Sarasvatī. His *dīkṣā-guru* was the supremely worshipable Śrīmad Gaurakiśora dāsa Bābājī Mahārāja. In Śrīman Mahāprabhu's birthplace of Śrī Dhāma Māyāpura he established his original monastery (*maṭha*), the Śrī Caitanya Maṭha. He went on to establish approximately sixty-four *maṭhas* in Bengal, Bihar, Orissa, Madras, Mumbai, Delhi, Uttar Pradesh and throughout the whole of India, as well as in Western and Eastern countries. In these he taught educated and cultured youths the *premamayī* (saturated with divine love) instructions of Śrīman Mahāprabhu. Attracting them by his heart-touching instructions and his ideal devotional character, he initiated them into the renounced order (*tridaṇḍa-sannyāsa*), sent them to preach both domestically and internationally, and inspired them to publish spiritual journals in various languages.

He also established the Vaiṣṇava system of occupational duties known as *daiva-varṇāśrama*. Travelling throughout India, with profound enthusiasm he preached *śuddha-bhakti* and inspired others to do the same. By publishing his own devotional books and periodicals as well as Upaniṣads, Purāṇas, the *Brahma-sūtra*, *Śrīmad-Bhāgavatam*, *Bhagavad-gītā*, the books of the Gosvāmīs and authoritative books of the four *sampradāyas*, he further expanded the enormous storehouse of Śrī Gauḍīya devotional literature. The world will remain forever indebted to this great personality.

My supremely worshipable Śrī Gurudeva, the crest jewel of topmost swan-like (*paramahaṁsa*) Vaiṣṇavas, Śrī Śrīmad Bhakti Prajñāna Keśava Gosvāmī Mahārāja, is a guardian of the Śrī Gauḍīya *sampradāya* and founding preceptor (*ācārya*) of the Gauḍīya Vedānta Samiti and all the *maṭhas* throughout India under its jurisdiction. Besides publishing his own books, he re-published many of Bhaktivinoda Ṭhākura's writings. By his special mercy and inspiration, devotional literatures are steadily being published by the Gauḍīya Vedānta Samiti. By his mercy, this English edition of *Śrī Upadeśāmṛta* is now being presented before our exalted readers.

This edition is a direct translation of the Hindi edition of *Śrī Upadeśāmṛta* which was first published by the Gauḍīya Vedānta Samiti in 1984. It was translated and edited through the combined efforts of Śrīman Navadvīpa dāsa Adhikārī and Śrīman Prema-vilāsa dāsa Adhikārī, who also designed the book and oversaw its publication. The final manuscript was proofread by Śrīmatī Yaśodā-gopī dāsī. I commend them all for their excellent work.

In providing word-for-word synonyms for the verses of *Śrī Upadeśāmṛta*, we have not followed the sequential order of the words as they appear in the verses but, rather, the natural order of the words as they appear in a sentence. This system is called *anvaya* in Sanskrit. *Anvaya* literally means the natural order or connection of words in a sentence. The meaning of the verse becomes self-evident by the *anvaya* system. We hope that the readers will appreciate the advantage of this system, as it helps one to delve deeper into the meaning of the verses. To bring this to the readers' attention in the book, we have identified the word-for-word synonyms simply as *anvaya*.

I am fully confident that by reading this book, faithful persons who are desirous of *bhakti* will become qualified to obtain the *prema-dharma* taught by Śrī Caitanya Mahāprabhu and that venerable devotees will be greatly delighted. May Śrī Śrī Guru-Gaurāṅga-Rādhā-Vinoda-bihārījī bestow Their plentiful, merciful blessings upon us. At Their lotus feet I offer this humble prayer (from Śrīla Raghunātha dāsa Gosvāmī's *Śrī Mukta-caritam*, Concluding Prayers 1):

ādadānas tṛṇaṁ dantair
idaṁ yāce punaḥ punaḥ
śrīmad rūpa-padāmbhoja
dhūliḥ syāṁ janma-janmani

"Clasping a straw between my teeth, repeatedly I beg to obtain the dust of Śrīla Rūpa Gosvāmī's lotus feet birth after birth."

A servant of the servant of the Vaiṣṇavas,

Tridaṇḍi-bhikṣu Śrī Bhaktivedānta Nārāyaṇa

Śrī Rūpa-Sanātana Gauḍīya Maṭha
Vṛndāvana, Uttar Pradesh, India
November 14, 1997, the final day
of the holy month of Kārttika.

Śrī Śrīmad Bhaktivedānta Nārāyaṇa Mahārāja

Śrī Guru Gaurāṅgau Jayataḥ

Verse One

Six Urges Unfavourable to Bhakti and Worthy of Rejection

वाचो वेगं मनसः क्रोधवेगं
जिह्वावेगमुदरोपस्थवेगम् ।
एतान् वेगान् यो विषहेत धीरः
सर्वामपीमां पृथिवीं स शिष्यात् ॥१॥

vāco vegaṁ manasaḥ krodha-vegaṁ
jihvā-vegam udaropastha-vegam
etān vegān yo viṣaheta dhīraḥ
sarvām apīmāṁ pṛthivīṁ sa śiṣyāt (1)

Anvaya

dhīraḥ–a wise and self-controlled person, free from desires for material enjoyment, liberation and mystic perfection; *yaḥ*–who; *viṣaheta*–can subdue; *etān*–all these; *vegān*–overwhelming passions; *vāco vegam*–the impetus of speech; *manasaḥ vegam*–the agitation of the mind; *krodha vegam*–the onset of anger; *jihvā vegam*–the vehemence of the tongue; *udara vegam*–the urge of the belly; *upastha vegam*–(and) the agitation of the genitals; *saḥ*–he; *śiṣyāt*–can instruct; *imām*–this; *sarvām*–entire; *pṛthivīm*–world; *api*–even

Translation

A wise and self-composed person who can subdue the impetus to speak, the agitation of the mind, the onset of anger, the vehemence of the tongue, the urge of the belly and the agitation of the genitals can instruct the entire world. In other words, all persons may become disciples of such a self-controlled person.

Maṅgalācaraṇa

I first of all offer repeated obeisances (*praṇāmas*) unto my most worshipable *śrī-gurudeva*, *nitya-līlā-praviṣṭa oṁ viṣṇupāda aṣṭottara-śata* Śrī Śrīmad Bhakti Prajñāna Keśava Gosvāmī, unto my *parama-gurudeva*, Śrī Śrīmad Bhaktisiddhānta Sarasvatī Gosvāmī 'Prabhupāda', who wrote the *Anuvṛtti* commentary, unto my *parātpara-gurudeva*, Śrī Śrīmad Bhaktivinoda Ṭhākura, who wrote the *Pīyūṣa-varṣiṇī* commentary, unto Śrī Rādhā-ramaṇa dāsa Gosvāmī, the servant of the Śrī

Rādhā-ramaṇa Deity, who wrote the *Upadeśa-prakāśikā-ṭīkā*, unto Śrī Rūpa Gosvāmī, who wrote this *Śrī Upadeśāmṛta* and whose only wealth is the conjugal mellow of devotion (*śṛṅgāra-rasa*), and to his worshipable Deity, Śrī Caitanya Mahāprabhu, who is decorated with the inner sentiment and bodily complexion of Śrī Rādhā. Falling at their feet again and again, I am beginning this translation of the *Upadeśa-prakāśikā-ṭīkā*.

Upadeśa-prakāśikā-ṭīkā

by Śrī Rādhā-ramaṇa dāsa Gosvāmī

Let there be all victory for Śrī Rādhā-ramaṇa. I offer prayers unto Śrī Caitanya Mahāprabhu, who is accompanied by the unfettered ascetic (*avadhūta*) Śrī Nityānanda Prabhu, the identical manifestation of Śrī Baladeva, by Śrī Advaita Ācārya, the incarnation of Mahā-Viṣṇu, by His potencies such as Śrī Gadādhara, and by His associates like Śrīvāsa. I take shelter of that Mahāprabhu, who is the fountainhead of all potencies of the world. I offer prayers with great respect and affection unto Śrī Rūpa Gosvāmī, whose entire wealth is *śṛṅgāra-rasa*. This means that the sole purpose of his life is to describe *śṛṅgāra-rasa*, also known as *unnatojjvala-prema-rasa*, the highest and most radiant divine love of Śrī Rādhā-Kṛṣṇa. He is always immersed in the service of the lotus feet of Śrī Rādhā-Govinda. He has purified all the living entities of this world by giving instructions on the methodology by which this type of *prema* may be obtained. I offer *praṇāma* unto Śrī Gopāla-bhaṭṭa Gosvāmī, who is very merciful to the destitute and wretched living entities who are enamoured with the external energy. I offer *praṇāma* once more unto the ocean of mercy Śrī Caitanya Mahāprabhu, the incarnation who sanctifies this Kali-yuga, who distributes *śrī-harināma* and love of God (*bhagavat-prema*) and who delivers the souls (*jīvas*) of this earth. I offer prayers unto Śrī Gopīnātha dāsa, a disciple of Śrī Gopāla-bhaṭṭa and servant of Śrī Rādhā-ramaṇa, who has benedicted innumerable living entities by bestowing *śrī-gaura-bhakti*. I offer *praṇāma* unto my *gurudeva*, Śrī Jīvana-lāla, of whom I am the grandson and servant. Offering *praṇāma* unto all of them, I am beginning this brief explanation of the verses of *Śrī Upadeśāmṛta*, written by Śrī Rūpa Gosvāmī for the benefit of the *sādhakas*.

In *Śrī Bhakti-rasāmṛta-sindhu*, Śrī Rūpa Gosvāmī has defined *uttamā-bhakti* as the cultivation of activities for

Śrī Kṛṣṇa, performed with a favourable mood which is devoid of all other desires and which is not covered by knowledge aiming at the oneness of the *jīvas* with the Lord (*jñāna*) or by fruitive activity (*karma*) which is not meant exclusively for the Lord's pleasure. How can such *uttamā-bhakti* manifest in persons whose hearts are filled with shortcomings such as lust and anger? In the *Padma Purāṇa* it is said:

śokāmarṣādibhir bhāvair
ākrāntaṁ yasya mānasam
kathaṁ tatra mukundasya
sphūrti sambhāvanā bhavet

"How can Śrī Mukunda ever be manifest to a person whose heart is invaded by lamentation, anger and other agitations?"

The purport of this statement is that when contaminations such as lust, anger and greed arise within the mind, the six overwhelming passions mentioned in the original verse cause the mind to become thoroughly engrossed in fleeting objects of sensual gratification. The cultivation of unalloyed *bhakti* is never possible in such a contaminated heart. Therefore, the instruction is given here to subdue these passions which impede the development of *bhakti*. The *sādhaka* who can tolerate these passions can instruct the entire world. The conclusion is that a *sādhaka* who has conquered his senses and subdued these passions can purify all the *jīvas* of the world by his resolute and pure *uttamā-bhakti*. Everyone may become the disciple of such a great personality.

In *Śrīmad-Bhāgavatam* (11.14.24) it is said:

vāg gadgadā dravate yasya cittaṁ
rudatya bhīkṣṇaṁ hasati kvacic ca
vilajja udgāyati nṛtyate ca
mad bhakti yukto bhuvanaṁ punāti

"My dear Uddhava! My devotee whose voice becomes choked up with *prema*, whose heart softens and begins to flow with spiritual emotion, who cannot cease from crying even for an instant, who sometimes bursts into laughter, sometimes begins to sing very loudly, abandoning all shyness, and sometimes dances, purifies not only himself but the entire world."

It is essential to note here that by subduing the six passions described already, what is obtained is merely the qualification to enter the realm of *bhakti*. These are not direct limbs of devotional practice (*sādhana-bhakti*) but, rather, the doorway through which one may enter the realm of *bhakti*. Because *bhakti* is the self-manifest function of the Lord's internal potency (*svarūpa-śakti*), when it makes its appearance these six passions automatically become pacified.

Pīyūṣa-varṣiṇī-vṛtti (Commentary in the form of a nectarine shower)

by Śrī Bhaktivinoda Ṭhākura

śrī godruṁa-candrāya namaḥ

"Obeisances unto Śrī Caitanya Mahāprabhu, the moon of Śrī Godruma."

yat kṛpā-sāgarodbhūtam upadeśāmṛtaṁ bhuvi
śrī rūpena samānītaṁ gauracandraṁ bhajāmi tam

"I worship Śrī Gauracandra, the ocean of mercy from which arose a stream of nectar collected by Śrī Rūpa Gosvāmī and brought forth in this world as *Śrī Upadeśāmṛta*."

natvā grantha praṇetāraṁ ṭīkākāraṁ praṇamya ca
mayā viracyate vṛttiḥ 'pīyūṣa-pariveśanī'

"Bowing down with great humility, I offer *praṇāma* unto the author of *Śrī Upadeśāmṛta*, Śrī Rūpa Gosvāmī, and unto the commentator, Śrī Rādhā-ramaṇa dāsa Gosvāmī. Thus I begin this commentary which is an offering of nectar."

anyābhilāṣitā-śūnyaṁ jñāna-karmādy anāvṛtam
ānukūlyena kṛṣṇānuśīlanaṁ bhaktir uttamā
(*Bhakti-rasāmṛta-sindhu,* 1.1.11)

"The cultivation of activities which are meant exclusively for the pleasure of Śrī Kṛṣṇa, or in other words the uninterrupted flow of service to Śrī Kṛṣṇa, performed through all endeavours of the body, mind and speech, and through the expression of various spiritual sentiments (*bhāvas*), which is not covered by knowledge aimed at impersonal liberation (*jñāna*) and reward-seeking activity (*karma*), and which is devoid of all desires other than the aspiration to bring happiness to Śrī Kṛṣṇa, is called *uttamā-bhakti*, pure devotional service."

Adopting all those things mentioned in the above verse as favourable and renouncing all that is unfavourable, one adopts the cultivation of activities meant exclusively for the pleasure of Śrī Kṛṣṇa. It is this cultivation, or *bhagavat-anuśīlana*, which is the primary objective of persons intent on *bhajana*. The acceptance of that which is favourable and the rejection of that which is unfavourable are not direct limbs (*aṅgas*) of *śuddha-bhakti*. Rather, they are aspects of that faith which is characterised by surrender (*śaraṇāgati*) which in turn bestows qualification for *bhakti*. This is expressed as follows in the *Vaiṣṇava-tantra* (quoted in *Bhakti-sandarbha*, *Anuccheda* 236):

ānukūlyasya saṅkalpaḥ prātikūlyasya varjanam
rakṣiṣyatīti viśvāso goptṛtve varaṇaṁ tathā
ātma-nikṣepa-kārpaṇye ṣaḍ-vidhā śaraṇāgatiḥ

"There are six symptoms of self-surrender: (1) *Ānukūlyasya saṅkalpa*–fully surrendered *sādhakas* should accept only those things which are favourable for *prema-bhakti*. (2) *Prātikūlya vivarjana*–they should completely reject those things which are unfavourable to *prema-bhakti*. (3) *Rakṣiṣyatīti viśvāsa*–they have firm faith that Śrī Kṛṣṇa is their only protector, that there is no protector other than Kṛṣṇa, and that one cannot obtain protection by any other activity. (4) *Goptṛtve varaṇa*–surrendered devotees have absolutely no doubt that Kṛṣṇa is their only guardian and maintainer. (5) *Ātma-nikṣepa*–offering the self to the Lord is expressed in this attitude: 'I am incapable of doing anything independently. Unless Kṛṣṇa desires, no one can do anything.' Devotees who have no other resort (*ātma-nikṣepa*) have this kind of faith. (6) *Kārpaṇya*–humility is expressed as follows: 'I am very fallen and insignificant.' Unalloyed devotees are possessed of this very firm and simple faith. To possess all these attitudes is called *śaraṇāgati*."

In this verse the instruction is given to abandon that which is unfavourable. One who is able to tolerate the overwhelming passions of speech, mind, anger, tongue, belly and genitals can instruct the entire world.

In the *Padma Purāṇa* it is said:

śokāmarṣādibhir bhāvair
ākrāntaṁ yasya mānasam
kathaṁ tatra mukundasya
sphūrti-sambhāvanā bhavet

"How can Śrī Mukunda ever be manifest to a person whose heart is invaded by lamentation, anger and other agitations?"

The purport of this verse is that lust, anger, greed, illusion, intoxication, envy and other irritations always arise within the mind and thus attract the mind towards material sense objects. This is effected through six agencies: (1) by the urge to speak or the use of words which create distress for others, (2) by the agitation of the mind or the innumerable desires and plans fabricated within the mind, (3) by anger or the use of harsh words, (4) by the vehemence of the tongue or the greed to relish six kinds of taste, namely sweet, sour, bitter, pungent, salty and astringent, (5) by the urge of the belly or the drive to eat more than necessary, and (6) by the agitation of the genitals or the desire for co-habitation between men and women. Therefore, the cultivation of *śuddha-bhakti* is not possible. In order to make the hearts of those who are pursuing the path of *bhajana* intent on *bhakti*, Śrī Rūpa Gosvāmī has composed this verse first.

The attempt to restrain these six urges does not constitute *bhakti-sādhana*, rather it is a staircase to ascend to the platform of eligibility through which one may enter the temple of *bhakti*. On the paths of fruitive activity (*karma*) and the cultivation of knowledge (*jñāna*) one is instructed to curb these six urges. These instructions, however, are not applicable for pure devotees. In the scriptures, hearing, chanting and remembrance of the names, form, qualities and pastimes of Śrī Kṛṣṇa are described as actual *bhakti*.

These six urges present various types of obstacles in the immature stage for the practitioner entering the path of *bhakti*. At that time the devotee, by taking shelter of the mood of exclusive *śaraṇāgati* and by avoiding the ten kinds of offences to the holy names (*nāmāparādha*), becomes fit to dispel these obstacles through the power of *harināma-kīrtana* and so on. The association of spotless saints (*sādhus*) plays a very significant role in this matter, as expressed in the *Padma Purāṇa*:

śrutvāpi nāma-māhātmyaṁ
yaḥ prītirahito 'ghamaḥ
ahaṁ namādi paramo
nāmni so 'py aparādha-kṛt

"Those who, in spite of hearing the astonishing glories of the holy name, maintain the conception that 'I am this material body' and that worldly objects are 'mine' and who display no persistence in or love for the utterance of the holy name are also offenders to the holy name."

The devotees are intent on practical renunciation (*yukta-vairāgya*) and thus they remain aloof from dry renunciation. Therefore, the regulation to abandon all contact with the sense objects does not pertain to them. When the agitation of the mind is withdrawn or, in other words, when one is devoid of thirst for material enjoyment, the impetuosity of the eyes, the life air, the hearing propensity and all other drives become pacified.

Therefore, persons who have gained victory over these six overwhelming passions can conquer the entire world. The instruction to tolerate these urges is given only for householder devotees, because before giving up householder life one must first have abandoned all types of urges.

Anuvṛtti

by Śrī Bhaktisiddhānta Sarasvatī Gosvāmī 'Prabhupāda'

The supremely compassionate Śrī Śacīnandana Gaurahari, who purifies the fallen souls, displayed unlimited mercy towards the *jīvas*, who are ravaged by the influence of Kali and averted from the service of Śrī Kṛṣṇa, by manifesting the instructions known as *Śrī Śikṣāṣṭaka*. In these verses He has very succinctly propounded in the form of codes all the instructions regarding the truths of *sambandha*,[1] *abhidheya*[2] and *prayojana*[3] for the living entities. His most beloved Śrī Rūpa Gosvāmī heard all these extremely confidential truths of devotional tenets (*bhakti-tattva*) from His lotus mouth at Jagannātha Purī and Prayāga. Not only did he hear these teachings, but the all-powerful embodiment of *prema*, Śrī Caitanya Mahāprabhu, invested his heart with the potency by which he could realise these confidential truths of *bhakti*. Śrī Rūpa Gosvāmī revealed these instructions in simple and straightforward Sanskrit language in his books such as *Śrī Bhakti-rasāmṛta-*

---

[1]*Sambandha* is the principle regarding the mutual relationships between the Lord, the living entities, and the material energy.

[2]*Abhideya* is the means by which the ultimate goal is achieved, in other words, the practices of *sādhana-bhakti*.

[3]*Prayojana* is the ultimate goal of devotional life, *kṛṣṇa-prema*.

sindhu, *Ujjvala-nīlamaṇi*, *Lalita-mādhava*, *Vidagdha-mādhava*, *Stava-mālā* and others. These sacred jewels of literature are a mine of good fortune filled with the priceless gems of *prema*. *Śrī Upadeśāmṛta* is one such invaluable jewel of *prema*. It is a necklace for the devotees of Mahāprabhu (*gaura-bhaktas*). Śrī Rūpa Gosvāmī collected the essence of all the instructions of Śrī Caitanya Mahāprabhu and offered it as a gift to the genuine *sādhakas*.

In *Śrī Upadeśāmṛta* two kinds of instruction are given. The first is to give up things which are unfavourable to *bhakti*, and the second is to adopt things which are favourable to *bhakti*. As long as the *sādhaka* fails to apply these two kinds of instructions in his life, there is no possibility that *bhāva-bhakti*[4] will manifest in his heart, what to speak of *prema-bhakti*.[5] At present there are many persons who adhere to various

---

[4]In *Bhakti-rasāmṛta-sindhu* (1.3.1), *bhāva* is defined as follows: "*Bhāva-bhakti* is a special manifestation of the potency of unalloyed goodness (*śuddha-sattva*). In other words, the constitutional characteristic of *bhāva-bhakti* is that it is a phenomena entirely constituted of *śuddha-sattva*. It is like a ray (*kiraṇa*) of the sun of *prema* and it softens the heart by various tastes (*ruci*)."

types of fabricated views, to doctrines which display only an external veneer of religion but which are actually opposed to *bhakti*, to ideas which are contrary to the Vedas, to opportunistic views, and to the doctrines of imitationism (*sahajiyā*), impersonalism (*māyāvāda*) and other diverse and contrary opinions. All such persons fear the instructions given in the form of this *Upadeśāmṛta*, considering them to be the personification of Yamarāja or he who administers punishment to the deceased. But faithful persons who study and recite this *Upadeśāmṛta* with great love and apply it in their lives will become free from all kinds of doubt in regard to *bhakti* and will easily attain first *bhāva-bhakti* and finally the most rare *prema-bhakti*. Therefore, holding the dust of the lotus feet of the *gurus* following in the line of Śrī Rūpa Gosvāmī upon my head, this Śrī Varṣabhānavī-dayitā dāsa, the servant of the lord of the life (*prāṇanātha*) of Vṛṣabhānu-nandinī Śrīmatī Rād-

[5] In *Bhakti-rasāmṛta-sindhu* (1.4.1), *prema* is defined as follows: "*Bhāva-bhakti* which melts the heart much more so than in its initial stage, which greatly augments the feeling of transcendental bliss, and which bestows a deep sense of possessiveness (*mamatā*) in relationship to Śrī Kṛṣṇa is called *prema* by the learned."

hikā, is setting down this commentary of *Śrī Upadeśāmṛta* named *Anuvṛtti*. The purpose of doing so is to immerse the *jīvas* in *Śrī Bhakti-rasāmṛta-sindhu*, which was revealed by Śrī Rūpa Gosvāmī and which was taught and carried out by the Vaiṣṇava preceptors who follow Śrī Rūpa (*rūpānuga-vaiṣṇava-ācāryas*), such as Śrī Gaurakiśora dāsa Bābājī and Śrī Bhaktivinoda Ṭhākura.

There are three kinds of overwhelming passions observed in worldly living entities attached to material sense enjoyment: the urges of speech, mind and body. When one falls into the powerful current of these three impetuous demands, it is very difficult to gain deliverance. Falling into the stream of repeated birth and death, such living entities are deprived of their spiritual well-being. But self-controlled persons who tolerate these demands are not overwhelmed by material sense enjoyment. They are competent to vanquish this material world.

The demands of speech refer to the speculations of the followers of impersonalism (*nirviśeṣa-vādīs*) which are opposed to *bhakti*, to the logical deliberations of the result-oriented workers ensnared in material activities which stress the fruits of action, and to all talk not related to the service of Śrī Kṛṣṇa but related to varieties of desire for material enjoyment. The demands of speech do not refer to those words which apply to the service of the Lord. On the contrary, such talks should be considered as the fruit of tolerating the demands of speech. Sometimes, although one adopts a vow of silence, he expresses desires for material enjoyment and so on simply by his bearing or by writing. These are also included within the demands of speech.

The agitations of the mind are of two types: (1) *avirodha prīti*–unimpeded attachment, and (2) *virodha-yukta krodha*–anger arising from impediments. Attachment for the faith of the *māyāvādīs*, veneration towards the adherence to result-oriented activity, and belief in the ideas of those who have many desires not related to the service of Kṛṣṇa are three kinds of *avirodha prīti*. Mere indifference to the activities of the *jñānīs*, *karmīs* and persons possessing other desires is but the unmanifest or undeveloped stage of unimpeded attachment. When there is an impediment to the fulfilment of material desires, when one fails to obtain the cherished fruit of one's work, and when in spite of all endeavour one does not obtain liberation (*mukti*), anger comes about. To meditate upon the pastimes of Śrī Kṛṣṇa is not a form of mental agitation, rather it is the means by which all mental agitation becomes pacified.

The demands of the body are also of three types: the urges of the tongue, belly and genitals. Anxiousness to relish any of the six kinds of taste and greed to enjoy animal flesh, fish, eggs, wine, excessive ghee, milk, *rabaḍī* (a condensed milk-sweet), cream and so on is known as the impetuosity of the tongue. *Sādhus* also avoid eating foods which are overly bitter or spiced with hot chili. Consumption of betel nut, the mixture of betel with various spices (*pāna*), cigarettes, marijuana, hemp, opium and other intoxicating substances, as well as onions and garlic, are also counted as impetuous demands of the tongue. *Sādhakas* of *bhakti* must never indulge in these intoxicants. One should very carefully save oneself from the vehemence of the tongue by honouring the food remnants (*mahā-prasāda*) of Bhagavān and His devotees. Although *mahā-prasāda* may be very tasteful, it is not included within the demands of the tongue. By honouring it with great faith one can conquer the demands of the tongue. But if on the pretext of accepting *prasāda* one desires one's own enjoyment and cunningly relishes its taste, that is also included as the passion of the tongue. To eat very costly and delicious food items such as *rabaḍī* and cream offered to the demigods (*devatās*) at the house of wealthy persons is detrimental for renounced (*niskiñcana*) Vaiṣṇavas. In order to satisfy the lust of the tongue one may become ensnared in various types of reprehensible behaviour and bad association. In *Śrī Caitanya-caritāmṛta* (*Antya-līlā* 6.227, 236), it is said:

jihvāra lālase jei iti utidhāya
śiśnodara-parāyaṇa kṛṣṇa nāhi pāya

bhāla na khāibe āra bhāla nā paribe

"Persons who are prone to carnal pleasure and eating too much and who run here and there to satisfy the greed of the tongue never obtain Śrī Kṛṣṇa. One should not wear elegant and expensive clothes, nor should one eat delicious-tasting food."

Sādhakas should very carefully avoid these things. Gluttonous persons usually suffer from different types of diseases. By eating too much, many difficulties ensue. Persons who eat excessively generally become subservient to the demands of the genitals and thus become debauchees. By accepting *bhagavat-prasāda* in a suitable manner, by observing Ekādaśī in accordance with the regulations and by serving Kṛṣṇa, the demands of the belly are mitigated.

The demands of the genitals are of two types: in accordance with scripture and not sanctioned by scripture. When a person who has attained maturity marries in accordance with scriptural regulations and observes the prescribed *dharma* for a householder (*gṛhastha*) by following the proper behavioural codes for begetting good progeny, he regulates the demand of the genitals. This is classified as sex indulgence in accordance with scripture. There are many different types of illicit sexual indulgence, such as transgressing scriptural and social codes and accepting another man's wife, lusting after eight types of conjugal exchanges and enjoying the senses by artificial and licentious means contrary to scriptural codes. Both householders and renunciates who are *sādhakas* of *bhakti* should always remain aloof from the demands of the tongue, belly and genitals.

In his book *Prema-vivarta* (7.3.1-4), the associate of Śrī Caitanyadeva, Śrī Jagadānanda Paṇḍita, has said:

vairāgī bhāī grāmya kathā nā śunibe kāne
grāmya-vārtā nā kahibe jabe milibe āne

svapne o nā kara bhāī strī sambhāṣaṇa
gṛhe strī chāḍiyā bhāī āsiyācha vana

yadi cāha praṇaya rākhite gaurāṅgera sane
choṭa haridāsera kathā thāke jena mane

bhāla nā khāibe āra bhāla nā paribe
hṛdayete rādhā-kṛṣṇa sarvadā sevibe

"O Vaiṣṇava mendicant, O brother, whomever you should meet, do not hear from him nor speak with him about mundane subjects. Do not speak intimately with a woman even in your dreams. O brother! You should give up your wife and household and retire to the forest. If you wish to develop love for the lotus feet of Śrī Śacīnandana Gaurahari, then you should always remember the example of Choṭa Haridāsa. If you desire *bhagavad-bhakti*, then you should not eat delicious food nor dress yourself very luxuriously. In this way you should always serve Śrī Rādhā-Kṛṣṇa within your heart."

Only one who is fully able to tolerate the six urges of body, mind and words which have already been described is fit to be addressed by the title of 'Gosvāmī', or one who is the master of his senses. Such *gosvāmīs* are the true servants of Śrī Kṛṣṇa. Those who, on the contrary, are controlled by these six demands should be called *go-dāsa*, servant or slave of the senses, and not *gosvāmī*.

Those who are *go-dāsa*, or servants of the senses, are actually servants of the illusory energy (*māyā*). If, therefore, they desire to become servants of Kṛṣṇa, they should follow in the footsteps of those who are truly *gosvāmīs*. There is no means other than this. Those whose senses are not controlled can never become devotees of Śrī Hari. In *Śrīmad-Bhāgavatam* (7.5.30), Śrī Prahlāda Mahārāja has said:

matir na kṛṣṇe parataḥ svato vā
mitho 'bhipadyeta gṛhavratānām
adāntagobhir viśatāṁ tanisraṁ
punaḥ punaś carvita carvaṇānām

"O Father, materialistic persons are simply milling over that which has already been milled and chewing that which has already been chewed. Because their senses are not controlled they are proceeding towards the dreadful hell of this material existence, repeatedly trying to enjoy that which has already been consumed. The intelligence of such materially attached persons cannot be turned towards Bhagavān Śrī Kṛṣṇa either by their own endeavour, by the instruction of others or by the association of similar materialistic persons."

Verse Two

Six Impediments to Bhakti

अत्याहारः प्रयासश्च प्रजल्पो नियमाग्रहः ।
जनसङ्गश्च लौल्यञ्च षड्भिर्भक्तिर्विनश्यति ॥२॥

atyāhāraḥ prayāsaś ca
prajalpo niyamāgrahaḥ
jana-saṅgaś ca laulyaṁ ca
ṣaḍbhir bhaktir vinaśyati (2)

Anvaya

atyāhārāḥ–eating too much or accumulating more than necessary; *prayāsaḥ*–endeavours opposed to bhakti; *ca*–and; *prajalpaḥ*–unessential and mundane talks; *niyamāgrahaḥ*–abandoning the rules prescribed for one's eligibility and adopting those rules which are meant for others; *ca*–and; *jana-saṅgaḥ*–association with worldly and sensualistic persons, association with women or men who are attached to women, association with māyāvādīs, atheists and other nondevotees; *ca*–and; *laulyam*–greed or the restlessness of the mind to adopt worthless opinions; *ṣaḍbhiḥ*–by these six faults; *bhaktir*–pure devotion; *vinaśyati*–is destroyed

Translation

Bhakti is destroyed by the following six kinds of faults: (1) eating too much or collecting more than necessary, (2) endeavours which are opposed to *bhakti*, (3) useless mundane talks, (4) failure to adopt essential regulations or fanatical adherence to regulations, (5) association with persons who are opposed to *bhakti*, and (6) greed or the restlessness of the mind to adopt worthless opinions.

Upadeśa-prakāśikā-ṭīkā

In the beginning stage of the practice of *bhakti* the material proclivity is prominent in the hearts of the *sādhakas*. Therefore, they are unable to subdue the six overwhelming passions described in the first verse. Consequently, in this condition, many tendencies develop in the heart of the *sādhakas* which are very harmful to *bhakti*. In this verse those injurious tendencies are being described for the benefit of the *sādhakas*. The word *atyāhāra* means to eat more than required or to accumulate material objects. The word *prayāsa* means to endeavour for worldly objects or to be engaged in activities which are opposed to *bhakti*. The word *prajalpa* means to uselessly criticise and gossip about others, which is a gross misuse of time. The word *niyamāgraha*, when broken into its constituent parts, has two meanings: (1) *niyama* + *āgraha*–over-zealousness in following rules, and (2) *niyama* + *agraha*–failure to accept rules. When the first meaning is applied, it refers to enthusiasm for those rules which yield an inferior result, such as promotion to the heavenly planets, leaving aside the endeavour for the superior attainment of the service of the Lord. When the second meaning is applied, it refers to indifference towards those rules which nourish *bhakti*. The words *jana-saṅga* mean to give up the association of pure devotees and keep company with others. In the conversation between Devahūti and Kardama Muni in the *Śrīmad-Bhāgavatam* (3.23.55), there is a very nice instruction about giving up worldly association:

saṅgo yaḥ saṁsṛter hetur
asatsu vihito 'dhiyā
sa eva sādhuṣu kṛto
niḥsaṅgatvāya kalpate

"O Deva! Association is the cause of both material bondage and liberation from material existence. When due to ignorance one keeps company with worldly-minded persons who are diverted from the path of *bhakti*, that association brings about one's material entanglement. When, however, one keeps company with pure devotees of the Lord, that association liberates one from material existence and causes one to obtain the lotus feet of the Lord."

Furthermore, Bhagavān Kapiladeva gives the following instructions to Devahūti:

saṅgaṁ na kuryāt pramadāsu jātu
yogasya pāraṁ paraṁ āruruksuḥ
mat-sevayā pratilabdhātma-lābho
vadanti yā niraya-dvāram asya
(*Śrīmad-Bhāgavatam* 3.31.39)

"Those who desire to obtain *kṛṣṇa-prema*, which is the ultimate fruit of *bhakti-yoga*, should never indulge in illicit association with women. Learned sages who know the absolute truth say that for those who desire liberation from material existence and attainment of the lotus feet of the Lord, illicit connection with women opens wide the door to hell."

teṣv aśānteṣu mūḍheṣu
khaṇḍitātmasv asādhuṣu
saṅgaṁ na kuryāc chocyeṣu
yoṣit-krīḍā-mṛgeṣu ca
(*Śrīmad-Bhāgavatam* 3.31.34)

"One should never associate with foolish, agitated, materialistic men who identify the body as the self, who are most deplorable, and who are dancing dogs in the hands of women."

Having pointed out the defects of material association, the revealed scriptures (*śāstra*) forbid it. The agitation of the mind for compatible objects and the unsteadiness of the mind which results from associating with persons of many different opinions is known as *laulya.* Such unsteadiness of the mind is like an unchaste woman wandering sometimes upon the path of *karma*, sometimes on the path of *yoga*, sometimes on the path of *jñāna* and sometimes upon the path of *bhakti.* By this the predilection for *bhakti* is destroyed.

Pīyūṣa-varṣiṇī-vṛtti

Atyāhāra, *prayāsa*, *prajalpa*, *niyamāgraha*, *jana-saṅga* and *laulya* are six faults which are directly opposed to *bhakti*. (1) The word *atyāhāra* is a compound word formed by combination of the prefix *ati*, which means too much or excessively, with the word *āhāra*, which means to seize, grasp or consume for one's own enjoyment. Excessive enjoyment of sense objects through any one of the senses and the endeavour to accumulate in excess of one's requirements are known as *atyāhāra*. Devotees who have renounced householder life are forbidden to accumulate material goods. *Gṛhastha* Vaiṣṇavas must acquire goods sufficient for their maintenance, but if they accumulate beyond their needs it is known as *atyāhāra*. Those who are eager to perform *bhajana* should not accumulate worldly goods like materialistic sense enjoyers. (2) The word *prayāsa* refers to activities which are opposed to *bhakti* or those which are performed for the enjoyment of the senses. (3) To waste time in useless, mundane talks is called *prajalpa*. (4) The word *niyamāgraha* has two meanings. When one has obtained a progressively higher qualification but remains over-zealous to adhere to the rules pertaining to a lower qualification, it is known as *niyama-āgraha*. Failure to observe the rules which nourish *bhakti* or, in other words, an absence of firm faith is known as *niyama-agraha*. (5) To associate with persons other than Bhagavān's devotees is known as *jana-saṅga*. (6) The word *laulya* means both unsteadiness and greediness. In the first sense it refers to the fickleness of the mind to accept many different kinds of false doctrines or uncertain conclusions. In the second sense it refers to attachment for worthless material sense enjoyment. By *prajalpa* one indulges in criticising *sādhus*, and by *laulya* one awakens a taste for many different temporary, uncertain conclusions. Both of these lead to *nāmāparādha*. Therefore, one should very carefully give them up.

Anuvṛtti

Excessive acquisition of knowledge which is the preoccupation of the *jñānīs*, accumulation of the fruits of work which is undertaken by the fruitive workers, and amassing too many material objects which is the business of those who are plagued with many desires are all known as *atyāhāra*. The cultivation of knowledge which is taken up by *jñānīs*, austerities and vows undertaken by *karmīs* and hard labour which is done by those possessed of many desires to obtain wife, children and wealth are called *prayāsa*. The dry scholarship of the *jñānīs* which amounts to nothing more than useless scriptural argumentation, praise of the benefits of pious deeds which generates fondness for religious rituals in the *karmīs*, and the talks which are pleasing to the senses of those who are possessed of many desires are called *prajalpa*. To accept the rules of the *jñāna-śāstras* in order to obtain liberation is called *āgraha*, or over-zealousness. Attachment for the rules outlined in the scriptures promoting pragmatism (practical as opposed to idealistic results) with a desire for sensual enjoyment both in this world and the next is known as *niyama-āgraha*. Establishment of certain rules of conduct appropriate for one's own status in order to achieve immediate happiness as advocated by the utilitarians or those who promote the greatest happiness for the greatest number is also known as *niyama-āgraha*. To remain indifferent to the rules which are prescribed for the attainment of *bhakti* is known as *niyama-agraha*. Such persons are so audacious that they try to pass off even their detestable wantonness and depravity as the most sacred and elevated path of spontaneous devotion (*rāga-mārga*). In *Hari-bhakti-vilāsa*, the disposition of such persons has been explained in the following words:

śruti-smṛti-purāṇādi
pañcarātra-vidhim vinā
aikāntikī harer bhaktir
utpātāyaiva kalpate

"Although engaged in single-minded devotion to Lord Hari, if one transgresses the regulations mentioned in the *śruti*, *smṛti*, Purāṇas and the *Nārada-pañcarātra*, great misgivings (*anarthas*) are produced."

In the *Kalyāṇa-kalpataru* also, Śrīla Bhaktivinoda Ṭhākura has said, "My dear mind, what have you done? Being in a very immature stage you have cheated yourself unknowingly by perpetrating the fault of narrow-mindedness upon the pure Vaiṣṇava *sampradāya*. You have supposed the pure conceptions and validity of the *sampradāya* to be hypocrisy and thus abandoned them. You have given up wearing the Vaiṣṇava *tilaka* markings and neck beads (*tulasī-mālā*) and put aside your chanting beads (*bhajana-mālā*). You think, 'What is the use of wearing *tilaka*? I can chant within my mind, so what need is there of beads? One's diet has nothing to do at all with *bhajana*. So don't think that you have to give up eating meat, fish or eggs. Don't think that you must stop drinking wine or tea and taking intoxicants such as *pāna*, tobacco, marijuana, hemp or opium.' You have cast aside the need for taking initiation (*dīkṣā*). You have begun to refer to yourself as an incarnation. You have begun to propagate your new theories very powerfully through different agents. You are criticising the opinions of the previous great personalities (*mahājanas*) and *ācāryas* of the path of *bhakti*, considering them to be mistaken. Some cunning persons put on *tilaka* and *tulasī-mālā* and cheat others. Therefore, you avoid the association of anyone who wears *tilaka* and *mālā*, considering them all to be cheaters. But, my dear brother mind, please consider, what have you gained by this? You have given up gold for ashes. Your present life and the next life have both been utterly ruined. You address everyone as a hypocrite, knave and cheater. But you have failed to attain *bhagavad-bhakti*. What will be your fate at the time of death?

"O mind, what should I tell you? You utter the words '*prema*, *prema*' but what good will it avail? *Prema* is a rare and priceless jewel. You will have to undertake arduous *sādhana* to attain it. By deceitful practice you make a show of tears, trembling, horripilation and fainting at the time of *kīrtana* or hearing spiritual discourses, yet your real business is simply to accumulate wealth, women and prestige. When you have not even a trace of attachment for pure *sādhana-bhakti* which is essential for the acquisition of *prema*, then how will you obtain such pure *bhagavat-prema*? You will have to first give up the ten offences against the holy name and chant *harināma* continuously. You should hear *hari-kathā* in the association of pure Vaiṣṇavas. Then, by the mercy of Śrī Nāma Prabhu, unalloyed *prema* will arise automatically in your heart.

"You have not performed *bhajana* in a regulated manner; you have not performed *saṅkīrtana* in the association of pure devotees. You have not withdrawn your mind from sense objects and engaged it in remembering the Lord in a secluded place. Without first climbing the tree, your attempt to pluck the fruit with your own hand has simply gone in vain. The most sacred and pure *kṛṣṇa-prema* is extremely rare. By misleading others you will simply cheat yourself. First make yourself fit by performing *sādhana*. Then *prema* will become easily accessible to you.

"O brother, although lust (*kāma*) and love (*prema*) appear identical by external indications, they are not at all the same. *Kāma* is like rusted iron, whereas *prema* is like pure gold. You have seized *kāma*, imagining it to be gold. Can anyone obtain *prema* by such absurd means?

"O foolish mind! You have become intoxicated by uselessly considering *kāma* to be *prema*. The lust for bones and flesh appears alluring for the time being. That lust chases endlessly after the objects of the senses. But unalloyed love is the natural disposition of the *jīva*. That *prema* is fully sentient and spiritual by nature. The object of that *prema* is Śrī Hari alone–not a dressed-up doll of bones and flesh. At present *prema* is in a dormant condition being covered by *kāma*. Therefore, you must endeavour to dispel this lust and to initiate the awakening of love.

"First, by good fortune due to the devotional pious credits (*sukṛti*) accumulated over many previous lifetimes, pure faith (*śraddhā*) arises. Then, by hearing *hari-kathā* and performing *harināma-kīrtana* in the association of pure devotees, *śraddhā* is matured and evolves successively into steadfastness (*niṣṭhā*), taste (*ruci*) and deep attachment (*āsakti*). From *āsakti*, *bhāva* makes its appearance, and from *bhāva*, *prema* is manifested. This is the order of development by which *prema* is awakened. *Prema* may be obtained only by taking support of this progressive evolution and never by any other means.

"O wicked mind! Why do you fear to take up this step-by-step method of *sādhana*? By mere imitation of *prema*, you will not obtain anything. By such an imitative display, you will attain only the temporary happiness of sense enjoyment which will also result in misery in the end. With this understanding, you should give up all offences and impediments (*anarthas*) and engage yourself in pure *sādhana-bhakti*. In this lies your good fortune."

The association of *jñānīs* whose aim is voidism or liberation, of fruitive workers who covet the fruits of their work, and of hedonistic enjoyers who are attached to sensual enjoyment, which is momentarily pleasing but ultimately culminates in distress, is known as *jana-saṅga*. When one obtains the association of Bhagavān's pure devotees, detrimental materialistic association automatically disappears.

The word *laulya* literally means greed or restlessness. This restlessness refers to the tendency of the mind to run after various pursuits with greed to taste their fruits.

With a desire to enjoy worldly sense enjoyment or to attain liberation, the mind sometimes runs in the direction of the eightfold *yoga* system, sometimes towards the process of meditation, sometimes towards the performance of sacrifices, and sometimes towards the practice by which one can attain impersonal *brahma*. This is known as *laulya*.

Thus one should give up the six kinds of faults–*atyāhāra*, *prayāsa*, *prajalpa*, *niyamāgraha*, *jana-saṅga* and *laulya*–and engage in pure *sādhana-bhakti*. If one fails to do so, then the power to understand that *kṛṣṇa-bhakti* bestows the highest good for all living entities will be covered over and one will be forever deviated from the path of *bhakti*.

Verse Three

Six Vows Favourable for Bhakti

उत्साहान्निश्चयाद्धैर्यात् तत्तत्कर्म-प्रवर्तनात् ।
संगत्यागात् सतोवृत्तेः षड्भिर्भक्तिः प्रसिध्यति ॥३॥

utsāhān niścayād dhairyāt
tat-tat-karma-pravartanāt
saṅga-tyāgāt sato vṛtteḥ
ṣaḍbhir bhaktiḥ prasidhyati (3)

Anvaya

utsāhāt–enthusiasm to carry out the rules which enhance bhakti; *niścayāt*–firm faith in the statements of the śāstra and the guru whose words are fully in line with the śāstra; *dhairyāt*–fortitude in the practice of bhakti, even in the midst of obstacles, or patience during the practice stage of bhakti even when there is delay in attaining one's desired goal; *tat-tat-karma-pravartanāt*–following the limbs of bhakti such as hearing and chanting and giving up one's material sense enjoyment for the pleasure of Śrī Kṛṣṇa; *saṅga-tyāgāt*–giving up illicit association with women, the association of those who are overly attached to women and the association of māyāvādīs, atheists and pseudo-religionists; *sato vṛtteḥ*–adopting the good behaviour and character of pure devotees; *ṣaḍbhiḥ*–by these six types of practice; *bhaktiḥ*–pure devotion; *prasidhyati*–is effected

Translation

Progress in *bhakti* may be obtained by the following six practices: (1) enthusiasm to carry out the rules which enhance *bhakti*, (2) firm faith in the statements of the *śāstra* and the *guru* whose words are fully in line with the *śāstra*, (3) fortitude in the practice of *bhakti*, even in the midst of obstacles, or patience during the practice stage of *bhakti*, even when there is delay in attaining one's desired goal, (4) following the limbs of *bhakti* such as hearing (*śravaṇa*) and chanting (*kīrtana*) and giving up one's material sense enjoyment for the pleasure of Śrī Kṛṣṇa, (5) giving up illicit connection with women, the association of those who are overly attached to women and the association of *māyāvādīs*, atheists and pseudo-religionists, and (6) adopting the good behaviour and character of pure devotees.

Upadeśa-prakāśikā-ṭīkā

The word *utsāhā*, or enthusiasm, refers to eagerness to perform the limbs of *sādhana* which enhance *bhakti*. The word *niścaya*, or conviction, signifies firm faith. *Dhairya* means not slackening one's execution of the limbs of *bhakti*, even when there is delay in obtaining the desired goal. The meaning of *tat-tat-karma-pravartanāt* is to fully renounce one's material enjoyment while endeavouring exclusively for the attainment of Bhagavān. In the *Śrīmad-Bhāgavatam* (11.19.24), Bhagavān Śrī Kṛṣṇa says to Uddhava:

evaṁ dharmair manuṣyāṇām
uddhavātma-nivedinām
mayi sañjāyate bhaktiḥ
ko 'nyo 'rtho 'syāvaśiṣyate

"Devotion which is saturated with love for Me arises in the hearts of those who offer their very souls unto Me and who follow the religious principles which are favourable for *bhakti*. What other object remains to be obtained for those who have attained My *bhakti*?"

The meaning of *sato-vṛtte* is to adopt the exalted conduct of devotees.

Pīyūṣa-varṣiṇī-vṛtti

Maintaining one's existence by appropriate means and cultivating *bhakti* are two essential activities for devotees. The first half of this verse indicates attitudes which are favourable for the cultivation of *bhakti* and the second half describes how a devotee should conduct his life. Enthusiasm, optimism, patience, executing activities which nourish *bhakti*, renouncing bad association and adopting the good behaviour of devotees are the means of obtaining success in *bhakti*.

(1) *Utsāha*–eagerness to follow the rules and regulations of *bhakti* is called *utsāha*. Without this enthusiasm, one's *bhakti* will vanish. Following the limbs of *bhakti* with great respect is real *utsāha*.

(2) *Niścaya*–the meaning of *niścaya* is firm faith.

(3) *Dhairya*–not slackening one's execution of the limbs of *bhakti*, even when there is delay in obtaining the desired goal, is called *dhairya*, or patience.

(4) *Bhakti-poṣaka-karma*–there are two types of activities which nourish *bhakti*: positive injunctions (*vidhi*) and negative injunctions (*niṣedha*). Performing the limbs of *bhakti*, headed by *śravaṇa* and *kīrtana*, is the prescribed *vidhi*. Renouncing one's personal enjoyment

for the purpose of giving pleasure to Śrī Kṛṣṇa is the primary *niṣedha*.

(5) *Saṅga-tyāga*–one should renounce the association of non-devotees, women and those attached to women. 'Non-devotees' here means sense-enjoyers, *māyāvādīs* and those who make a pretentious display of *dharma*.

(6) *Sad-vṛtti*–one should adopt the virtuous conduct of pure devotees and thereby maintain one's life in a suitable manner. Renunciate devotees should beg alms, preferably by performing *mādhukarī*. This is a process of begging where, like a *mādhukara* or bee taking nectar from many different flowers, they accept very little alms from many different households. Householder devotees should sustain their lives by means which are favourable to the regulations pertaining to the Vedic system of social order (*varṇāśrama*)–this is *sad-vṛtti*.

Anuvṛtti

Utsāha means to remain indifferent to the cultivation of *jñāna*, the activities of *karma*, *sādhanas* which have any aim other than to please Śrī Kṛṣṇa, and one's preferred variety of material enjoyment, while resolutely executing the limbs of *sādhana-bhakti*. "*Bhagavad-*

bhakti alone is the ultimate objective of all living beings"–such firm faith is called *niścaya.* Sometimes wandering onto the paths of *karma*, *jñāna* and so forth makes one's mind restless and following their *sādhanas* only produces suffering in the end. "Therefore, the path of *bhakti* is the sole constitutional path for all *jīvas*"–such firm conviction is called *dhairya*, or fortitude. The *Śrīmad-Bhāgavatam* (10.2.32-33) describes those *jñānīs* who commit offence at Bhagavān's lotus feet by falsely considering themselves liberated, and also the steadfastness of loving (*premī*) devotees upon the path of *bhakti*:

ye 'nye 'ravindākṣa vimukta-māninas
tvayy asta-bhāvād aviśuddha-buddhayaḥ
āruhya kṛcchreṇa paraṁ padaṁ tataḥ
patanty adho 'nādṛta-yuṣmad-aṅghrayaḥ

"O lotus-eyed Lord! Those who do not take shelter of Your lotus feet vainly consider themselves to be liberated. Because they are devoid of affection and devotion for You, their intelligence is impure. Even though such persons approach the platform of liberation by undergoing severe austerities and following spiritual practices, they fall from that position due to neglecting Your lotus feet."

tathā na te mādhava tāvakāḥ kvacid
bhraśyanti mārgāt tvayi baddha-sauhṛdāḥ
tvayābhiguptā vicaranti nirbhayā
vināyakānīkapa-mūrdhasu prabho

"O Mādhava, the *jñānīs* who imagine themselves to be liberated may fall from their so-called position of liberation, but Your devotees who are bound to You by a tie of intimate affection never fall from the path of *bhakti*. Because such devotees are fully protected by You, they fearlessly cross over all obstacles by placing their feet upon the heads of the predominating deities who are empowered to instigate the most severe types of obstacles."

Concerning the path of *bhakti*, Haridāsa Ṭhākura took a steadfast vow to chant in the face of all obstacles. This ideal in the realm of *bhakti* is related in this verse from *Caitanya-Bhāgavat* (*Ādi-līlā* 16.94):

khaṇḍa-khaṇḍa hai deha jāya yadi prāṇa
tabu āmi vadane nā chāḍi harināma

"Regardless if my body is cut to pieces and the life-air exits my body, I will never abandon the chanting of *harināma*."

Such determination to remain upon the path of *bhakti* is called *dhairya*, fortitude. To execute the limbs of *bhakti*, such as hearing *hari-kathā*, performing *kīrtana* of *bhagavat-nāma* and meditating on Bhagavān's names, form and pastimes with such determination, is *tat-tat-karma-pravartanāt*.

The association of Bhagavān's devotees is very desirable. One should never associate with *karmīs*, *jñānīs* or those who are filled with extraneous desires, knowing them to be less intelligent and of an enjoying tendency. What to speak of approaching them to fulfil any type of desire for prestige, to maintain any type of relationship with them is not proper. Keeping such bad association at a safe distance, one should adopt the ways of those saintly devotees who are always immersed in chanting *harināma*. *Karma*, *jñāna*, *aṣṭāṅga-yoga* and so forth, which are devoid of the desire to please Kṛṣṇa (*bhagavad-bhāva*), are not steps along the path of *bhakti*. Even if one possesses all good qualities, if he is devoid of *bhakti*, those very qualities merely transform into faults. But all virtuous qualities certainly reside within one who possesses *bhakti*. Therefore, the path of *bhakti* is characterised by saintly conduct.

Enthusiasm to serve Śrī Kṛṣṇa, full faith and steadfastness in that service, ensuring that all endeavours are solely for Kṛṣṇa's service, renouncing the company of all others except Kṛṣṇa's devotees and following in the footsteps of Kṛṣṇa's devotees–these six practices enhance *bhakti*.

Verse Four

Association Which Nourishes Bhakti

ददाति प्रतिगृह्णाति गुह्यमाख्याति पृच्छति ।
भुङ्क्ते भोजयते चैव षड्विधं प्रीतिलक्षणम् ॥४॥

dadāti pratigṛhṇāti
guhyam ākhyāti pṛcchati
bhuṅkte bhojayate caiva
ṣaḍ-vidhaṁ prīti-lakṣaṇam (4)

Anvaya

dadāti–offering pure devotees those objects which are in accordance with their requirements; *prati-gṛhṇāti*–accepting those prasādī or remnant items given by pure devotees; *guhyam ākhyāti*–revealing to devotees one's confidential realisations concerning bhajana; *pṛcchati*–inquiring from devotees about their confidential realisations; *bhuṅkte*–eating with great love the prasāda remnants given by devotees; *ca*–and; *bhoja-yate*–lovingly serving prasāda to devotees; *ca*–and; *ṣaḍ-vidham eva*–are specifically of these six kinds; *prīti-lakṣaṇam*–the symptoms of loving association with devotees

Translation

Offering pure devotees items in accordance with their requirements, accepting *prasādī* or remnant items given by pure devotees, revealing to devotees one's confidential realisations concerning *bhajana*, inquiring from them about their confidential realisations, eating with great love the *prasāda* remnants given by devotees and lovingly feeding them *prasāda*–these are the six symptoms of loving association with devotees.

Upadeśa-prakāśikā-ṭīkā

In this fourth verse, the extrinsic symptoms of loving exchanges with pure devotees are described. As the meaning of this verse is perfectly clear, it does not require elaboration.

Pīyūṣa-varṣiṇī-vṛtti

Bad association is unfavourable to *bhakti*; therefore, it is imperative to abandon such association. Those who are intent on progressing in *bhakti* should associate with pure devotees who possess the power to free one from the tendency to fall into bad association. A description of the loving exchanges shared between devotees which nourish one's *bhakti* is found in this fourth verse. Lovingly giving another devotee that which he requires and lovingly accepting those items which are mercifully given by other devotees, revealing one's confidential realisations to devotees and hearing descriptions of confidential tenets (*tattva*) from pure devotees, lovingly serving devotees *prasāda* and accepting *prasāda* offered by devotees–these six kinds of exchanges constitute association with saintly persons (*sādhu-saṅga*) in its pure form. These six activities are the symptoms of love. One should serve *sādhus* by the performance of these activities.

Anuvṛtti

Bhakti appears by the association of Bhagavān's devotees, but since one may not know how to associate with Vaiṣṇavas, this topic is explained in this verse. By the negative effect of maintaining affectionate relationships with the *jñānīs* who desire liberation from material existence, with the *karmīs* who desire to enjoy the fruits of their actions and with gross sense enjoyers, one's *bhakti* is harmed. One should not give these three types of persons any advice or any item. To do so would be offensive, because describing the glories of *harināma* to those devoid of faith is included within the category of *nāmāparādha*. Also one should never accept any advice regarding the attainment of liberation or material enjoyment from such persons, because it will lead one to develop affectionate attachment for them. One should not instruct them on how to perform *kṛṣṇa-bhajana*. One should not hear from them anything concerning the confidential aspects of *bhakti*. One should also not accept food which has been touched by them. By eating food prepared by them, their predilection for either material enjoyment or liberation will be transmitted within one's heart.

viṣayīra anna khāile malina haya mana
malina mana haile nahe kṛṣṇera smaraṇa
(*Śrī Caitanya-caritāmṛta*, *Antya-līlā* 6.279)

"When one eats food offered by a materialist, one's mind becomes contaminated. When the mind is contaminated, one is unable to remember Kṛṣṇa."

Therefore, one should not feed these three types of persons who possess an enjoying spirit. Eating food prepared by them or feeding them increases one's affection for them. Exchanging love with devotees who are of the same aspiration as oneself and who are affectionate to oneself enhances one's *bhakti.* Offering and accepting items, revealing confidential realisations to one another, and serving and accepting food are all activities which increase affection. One should not perform these activities with those of different aspirations in life than one's own.

Verse Five

Service Rendered by an Intermediate Devotee to the Three Kinds of Vaiṣṇavas

कृष्णेति यस्य गिरि तं मनसाद्रियेत
दीक्षास्ति चेत् प्रणतिभिश्च भजन्तमीशम् ।
शुश्रूषया भजनविज्ञमनन्यमन्य-
निन्दादिशून्यहृदमीप्सितसङ्गलब्ध्या ॥५॥

kṛṣṇeti yasya giri taṁ manasādriyeta
dīkṣāsti cet praṇatibhiś ca bhajantam īśam
śuśrūṣayā bhajana-vijñam ananyam anya-
nindādi-śūnya-hṛdam īpsita-saṅga-labdhyā (5)

Anvaya

ādriyeta–one should respect; *manasā*–within the mind; *tam*–that person (a neophyte devotee); *yasya giri*–in whose speech; *iti*–thus (appears); *kṛṣṇa*–one name of Kṛṣṇa; (one should offer respect) *praṇatibhiḥ*–by offering praṇāma; *ca*–also; *bhajantam*–an intermediate devotee who, being endowed with the correct understanding of reality and illusion, performs bhajana in accordance with the Vaiṣṇava conventions; *īśam*–Śrī Bhagavān; *cet*–if; *asti*–he has; *dīkṣā*–accepted initiation from a qualified guru; (and) *labdhyā*–having obtained; *īpsita-saṅga*–the association for which one hankers (the association of a topmost devotee whose heart is established in the particular mood of service to Śrī Rādhā-Kṛṣṇa for which one aspires and who is affectionately disposed towards oneself); *śuśrūṣayā*–with all types of service (such as offering daṇḍavat-praṇāma, making relevant inquiry and rendering service); (one should respect) *bhajana-vijñam*–a self-realised, expert mahā-bhāgavata Vaiṣṇava who performs bhajana of Śrī Rādhā-Kṛṣṇa's eightfold daily pastimes by rendering service mentally; *ananyam*–who is an exclusive devotee of Śrī Kṛṣṇa; *anya-nindādi-śūnya-hṛdam*–and whose heart, due to his undeviating absorption in Kṛṣṇa, is free from faults such as the tendency to criticise others

Translation

One who takes *kṛṣṇa-nāma* just once by calling out "O Kṛṣṇa!" is a neophyte devotee (*kaniṣṭha-adhikārī*). One should consider him to be his family member and silently respect him. One who, fully understanding the principle of *dīkṣā*, has accepted initiation from a qualified *guru* and performs *bhajana* of Bhagavān in accordance with the Vaiṣṇava conventions is an intermediate devotee (*madhyama-adhikārī*). One should respect such a devotee who is endowed with the correct understanding of reality and illusion by offering *praṇāma* unto him and so forth. One who is conversant with the science of *bhajana* as described in the *Śrīmad-Bhāgavatam* and other Vaiṣṇava scriptures and who performs exclusive *bhajana* of Śrī Kṛṣṇa is a *mahā-bhāgavata* devotee. Due to his undeviating absorption in Kṛṣṇa, the pure heart of such a devotee is free from faults such as the tendency to criticise others. He is expert in *bhajana*, meaning that he mentally renders service (*mānasa-sevā*) to Śrī Rādhā-Kṛṣṇa's pastimes which take place during the eight segments of the day (*aṣṭa-kālīya-līlā*). Knowing him to be a topmost devotee whose heart is established in the particular mood of service to Śrī Rādhā-Kṛṣṇa for which one aspires and who is affectionately disposed towards oneself, one should honour him by offering *daṇḍavat-praṇāma* (*praṇipāta*), making relevant inquiry (*paripraśna*) and rendering service (*sevā*) with great love.

Upadeśa-prakāśikā-ṭīkā

This verse gives instruction on *svarūpa-siddhā-bhakti.*[6] We should respectfully offer *praṇāma* to those who have accepted initiation from a qualified *guru*. In all ways we should lovingly serve those who perform exclusive *bhajana* of Śrī Kṛṣṇa by *mānasa-sevā* and who are expert in the procedure of worshipping Kṛṣṇa's *aṣṭa-kālīya-līlā*, knowing them to be the most desirable association. The meaning of "exclusive *bhajana*" is to be solely devoted to the worship of Śrī Rādhā-Kṛṣṇa in Vraja, without attachment for Lakṣmī-Nārāyaṇa or other incarnations of Bhagavān. It says in the *Śrī Bhakti-rasāmṛta-sindhu* that amongst the exclusive devotees of the many differ-

[6]All favourable endeavours (*ceṣṭā*) such as *śravaṇa*, *kīrtana*, *smaraṇa* and so on, as well as the manifestation of the spiritual sentiments which occur beginning from the stage of *bhāva*, which are completely devoid of all desires separate from Śrī Kṛṣṇa and which are freed from the coverings of *jñāna* and *karma*, are known as *svarūpa-siddhā-bhakti*. In other words, all endeavours of the body, words and mind which are related to Śrī Kṛṣṇa and which are performed exclusively and directly for His pleasure without any intervention are known as *svarūpa-siddhā-bhakti*.

ent incarnations of Bhagavān, those whose hearts have been stolen by Śrī Nanda-nandana are the best because even the favour of the master of Lakṣmī, Śrī Nārāyaṇa, cannot attract their minds. Because such exclusive devotees are forever alert to cultivate *bhakti* in the company of those topmost devotees who are expert in relishing devotional mellows (*rasika*), as well as being like-minded and affectionate, their hearts are always free from contaminations such as the tendency to criticise others. Knowing these topmost devotees to be the most desirable association, one should respect them mentally, offer *praṇāma* unto them and render service to them with great love.

Another meaning of this verse can be given. One should respect within the mind those who have accepted initiation from a qualified *guru* and chant *kṛṣṇa-nāma*. One should respect those who have accepted initiation from a bona fide spiritual master (*sad-guru*), who have developed an understanding of *sambandha-jñāna*[7] and who perform *bhajana* purely, by offering *praṇāma* to them and so forth. The best devo-

[7] *Sambandha-jñāna* is knowledge regarding *sambandha-tattva*, the mutual relationship between the Lord, the living entities and the material energy. The word *sambandha* means con-

tees are those who are devoid of the tendency to blaspheme others and who, being exclusively devoted to Śrī Rādhā-Kṛṣṇa, are forever alert to render service mentally to Their *aṣṭa-kālīya-līlā*. Knowing such devotees to be established in the particular mood of service to Śrī Rādhā-Kṛṣṇa for which one aspires, to be affectionately disposed towards oneself and to be the topmost association, one should honour them in all respects by offering *daṇḍavat-praṇāma* (*praṇipāta*), making relevant inquiry (*paripraśna*) and rendering service (*sevā*) with great affection. One should understand the eminence of Vaiṣṇavas according to this gradation.

In the original verse by Śrī Rūpa Gosvāmī, the word '*ādi*', meaning "and so forth", has been used after the word '*ninda*', which means to criticise. We should understand this to indicate envy, aggression and other faults which generally accompany the tendency to criti-

---

nection, relationship and binding. The living entities are eternally and inseparably connected to the Supreme Lord. Therefore, He is the true object of relationship. The general relationship between the living entities and the Supreme Lord is one of servant and served. However, in the perfectional stage of *bhakti*, one becomes established in a specific relationship with the Lord either as a servant, friend, parent or lover.

cise others. In the *Śrīmad-Bhāgavatam* (3.25.24), Kapiladeva says:

ta ete sādhavaḥ sādhvi
sarva-saṅga-vivarjitāḥ
saṅgas teṣv atha te prārthyaḥ
saṅga-doṣa-harā hi te

"O Sādhvi (virtuous lady)! The only desirable association is that of pure-hearted *sādhus* who always remain aloof from all varieties of bad association. By the influence of their association, the contaminations accrued through bad association can be eradicated."

Pīyūṣa-varṣiṇī-vṛtti

According to the instruction given in this verse, as long as a *sādhaka* remains within the *madhyama-adhikārī* stage, he is obliged to render service to devotees. The topmost devotee (*uttama-bhakta*) sees all living entities with equal vision. Therefore, he doesn't discriminate between devotees and non-devotees. The intermediate devotee (*madhyama-bhakta*) is one who sincerely endeavours to perform *bhajana*. This fifth verse indicates how *madhyama* devotees should behave towards the topmost class of devotees. If one remains aloof from the association of men who are attached to women, nondevotees and sense-enjoyers, their faults will not come within him. Still, understanding neophyte devotees (*kaniṣṭha-bhaktas*) to be ignorant due to their lack of knowledge of *sambandha-tattva*, the *madhyama* devotee should be merciful to them. Hearing such neophyte devotees uttering *kṛṣṇa-nāma*, a *madhyama* devotee will respect them within his mind. If a *kaniṣṭha* devotee accepts initiation and engages in *hari-bhajana*, a *madhyama* devotee will show him respect by offering *praṇāma* to him. Understanding the association of *mahā-bhāgavata* Vaiṣṇavas who are free from the tendency to criticise others to be most beneficial, one should honour them by rendering service to them. This service alone is the root cause of all spiritual perfections.

Anuvṛtti

In *Bhakti-sandarbha* (868), Śrī Jīva Gosvāmī defines the procedure known as *vaiṣṇava-dīkṣā* in the following statement:

divyaṁ jñānaṁ yato dadyāt
kuryāt pāpasya saṅkṣayam
tasmād dīkṣeti sā proktā
deśikais tattva-kovidaiḥ

"That process which bestows transcendental knowledge (*divya-jñāna*) and destroys sinful desires for material sense enjoyment is called *dīkṣā* by learned authorities in the absolute truth."

One should silently respect a devotee who, knowing that Śrī Kṛṣṇa and *śrī-kṛṣṇa-nāma* are nondifferent and transcendental and that *śrī-nāma* alone is the supreme object of worship and *bhajana*, takes exclusive shelter of *kṛṣṇa-nāma* and is devoted to chanting. Although the *mantras* which the disciple receives at the time of *dīkṣā* consist entirely of *śrī-nāma*, the names which form the basis of those *mantras* are endowed with specific knowledge of the disciple's relationship with the Lord. Without taking shelter of *harināma*, one cannot become *hari-jana* or a member of Kṛṣṇa's family. Śrī Caitanya Mahāprabhu determined the gradations in Vaiṣṇavas through showing the gradations in their faith in *hari-nāma*. One who has chanted *kṛṣṇa-nāma* just once is a (*kaniṣṭha*) Vaiṣṇava. One who constantly chants *kṛṣṇa-*

nāma is a superior (*madhyama*) Vaiṣṇava. The topmost Vaiṣṇava (*uttama* or *mahā-bhāgavata*) is he at the mere sight of whom others automatically begin chanting *kṛṣṇa-nāma*. One should respect the *kaniṣṭha* Vaiṣṇava within one's mind. One should respect the *madhyama* Vaiṣṇava by offering *praṇāma* to him and so forth. Knowing the *uttama* Vaiṣṇava to be the topmost devotee who is established in the particular mood of service to Śrī Rādhā-Kṛṣṇa for which one aspires and to be affectionately disposed towards oneself, one should serve him with great love.

(1) Because the *mahā-bhāgavata* devotees see everything as being related to Kṛṣṇa, they see all living entities with equal vision. Like *madhyama-adhikārī* devotees, they are intent on performing *bhajana*, and like *kaniṣṭha-adhikārī* devotees, they are devoted to chanting *harināma*.

(2) *Madhyama-adhikārīs* possess *prema* for Śrī Kṛṣṇa, and they respect the three levels of Vaiṣṇavas–*uttama*, *madhyama* and *kaniṣṭha*–by rendering service, offering *praṇāma* and offering respect within the mind, respectively. They always endeavour to turn the living entities who are averse to Kṛṣṇa towards Him. They are indifferent to those who are inimical to Him. They do not

see all living entities with equal vision as the *uttama-adhikārī mahā-bhāgavata* devotees do. If they fraudulently imitate the *mahā-bhāgavata* devotee, they will very quickly fall down from their position.

(3) The *kaniṣṭha-adhikārī* devotees take full shelter of the chanting of *śrī-kṛṣṇa-nāma*, knowing it to be supremely beneficial. But they don't realise that the position of the *madhyama-adhikārī* is above their present position and that they should strive to reach that position at sometime in the future. Sometimes the *kaniṣṭha-adhikārī* falls down due to considering himself a *guru*. Therefore, carefully giving appropriate respect to the *uttama* devotees, they should take full shelter of *śrī-nāma*.

Verse Six

It is Forbidden to View the Transcendental Vaiṣṇavas with Material Vision

दृष्टैः स्वभावजनितैर्वपुषश्च दोषैर्
न प्राकृतत्वमिह भक्तजनस्य पश्येत् ।
गङ्गाम्भसां न खलु बुद्बुदफेन पङ्कै-
र्ब्रह्मद्रवत्वमपगच्छति नीरधर्मैः ॥६॥

dṛṣṭaiḥ svabhāva-janitair vapuṣaś ca doṣair
na prākṛtatvam iha bhakta-janasya paśyet
gaṅgāmbhasāṁ na khalu budbuda-phena-paṅkair
brahma-dravatvam apagacchati nīra-dharmaiḥ (6)

Anvaya

na paśyet–one should not see or, in other words, should not consider a devotee to be an ordinary mundane person; *prākṛtatvaṁ dṛṣṭaiḥ*–seeing with material vision; *svabhāva-janitaiḥ*–due to the defects stemming from his nature, such as birth in a low caste, harshness, lethargy and so forth; *ca*–and; *doṣaiḥ*–due to the faults; *vapuṣaḥ*–of the body, such as ugliness, disease, deformities and so forth; *bhakta-janasya*–the devotee of Bhagavān; *iha*–situated in this world; *brahma-dravatvam*–(just as) the nature of liquified transcendence; *gaṅgāmbhasām*–of the water of the Ganges; *na khalu apagacchati*–is never lost; *budbuda-phena-paṅkaiḥ*–by the presence of bubbles, foam, mud and so forth; *nīra-dharmaiḥ*–which exist simply due to the nature of water

Translation

Devotees situated in this material world should not be viewed with material vision; in other words, one should not consider them to be ordinary conditioned souls. The imperfections visible in their natures, such as birth in a low caste, harshness, lethargy and so forth, and the imperfections visible in their bodies such as ugly features, disease, deformities and so forth, are precisely like the appearance of bubbles, foam and mud in the Ganges. Despite such apparent pollution in the water of the Ganges, she retains her nature as liquified transcendence. Similarly, the self-realised Vaiṣṇavas always exist on the transcendental plane and one should not attribute material defects to them.

Upadeśa-prakāśikā-ṭīkā

Due to their residing within the material world, pure devotees seem to have some apparent defects from the mundane perspective. Nevertheless, we should not consider such devotees to be material or, in other words, to be ordinary conditioned souls. If one notices imperfections in their natures, such as harshness, anger, greed and so forth, or imperfections in their bodies, such as lack of cleanliness, ugliness, aging and so forth, he should never assign mundane attributes to them. It is impossible for these mundane imperfections to exist within devotees' spiritually perfected bodies. Therefore, to perceive these mundane defects in elevated devotees is offensive. This point has been made clear by the example of Ganges water.

Pīyūṣa-varṣiṇī-vṛtti

The instruction of this sixth verse is that it is improper to perceive mundane defects in pure devotees and to consider them to be mere conditioned souls. It is impossible for pure devotees to fall into bad association and to commit offenses to the holy name. Perhaps there can be some imperfections in their bodies and in their natures. Lack of cleanliness, deformity, ugliness, old age and so forth are bodily imperfections. Birth in a low caste, harshness, lethargy and so forth are imperfections in one's character. The water of the Ganges is considered to be pure despite the natural appearance of bubbles, foam, mud and so on within it, and its nature as liquified transcendence is not lost. Similarly, Vaiṣṇavas who have realised their eternal identities are not contaminated by the natural transformations of the physical body such as birth, aging, death and so on. Therefore, even upon observing imperfections in a pure Vaiṣṇava, one intent on performing *bhajana* should never disrespect him. By disrespecting such a personality, one becomes an offender (*aparādhī*).

Anuvṛtti

One should not perceive the apparent defects in the bodies or characters of pure devotees by viewing such devotees with mundane vision. Just as the water of the Ganges forever remains transcendental though it is mixed with bubbles, foam and mud, similarly, pure devotees are always transcendental. To view them on the basis of mundane considerations is offensive. Śrī Kṛṣṇa, in *Bhagavad-gītā* (9.30-31), has also warned to beware of this:

api cet su-durācāro
bhajate mām ananya-bhāk
sādhur eva sa mantavyaḥ
samyag vyavasito hi saḥ

kṣipraṁ bhavati dharmātmā
śaśvac chāntiṁ nigacchati
kaunteya pratijānīhi
na me bhaktaḥ praṇaśyati

"If even the most ill-behaved person intently engages in exclusive devotional service unto Me, he is worthy of being considered a saintly person due to his intelligence being fixed on that devotion. He quickly becomes righteous and attains eternal peace. O son of Kunti! Attest that My devotee never perishes."

Even though a devotee of Kṛṣṇa may not be born in a *brāhmaṇa* family or a *gosvāmī* line, to not refer to him as 'Gosvāmī' or 'Prabhu' is considered viewing him with mundane vision. Devotees born in *gosvāmī* lines and those born in any other caste should be treated equally. Regardless of the caste in which a devotee has taken birth, to assign material attributes to him is offensive. But if any person who has made any degree of progress along the path of *bhakti* considers himself a devotee and begins engaging in material misconduct, he will certainly fall from the path of *bhakti*. By coming into contact with such persons, one's *bhakti* is destroyed.

Some people, being proud of their birth in a *brāhmaṇa* family or similarly high lineage, are unable to grasp either the impeccable conduct or the elevated spiritual thought of perfected devotees (*siddha-bhaktas*). Due to this, they disrespect Vaiṣṇavas in varieties of ways and become offenders at the feet of Vaiṣṇavas (*vaiṣṇava-aparādhīs*). Therefore, in this matter, *sādhakas* should remain very careful.

Verse Seven

The Process of Performing Bhajana of Śrī Kṛṣṇa's Name and Pastimes

स्यात् कृष्णनामचरितादि सिताप्यविद्या-
पित्तोपतप्तरसनस्य न रोचिका नु ।
किन्त्वादरादनुदिनं खलु सैव जुष्टा
स्वाद्वी क्रमाद्भवति तद्गदमूलहन्त्री ॥७॥

syāt kṛṣṇa-nāma-caritādi-sitāpy avidyā-
pittopatapta-rasanasya na rocikā nu
kintv ādarād anudinaṁ khalu saiva juṣṭā
svādvī kramād bhavati tad-gada-mūla-hantrī (7)

Anvaya

nu–aho!; *sitā api*–even the delightfully sweet sugar-candy; *kṛṣṇa-nāma-caritādi*–of Śrī Kṛṣṇa's names, form, qualities and pastimes; *na syāt*–is not; *rocikā*–tasteful; *rasanasya*–to the tongue; *upatapta*–which is afflicted; *pitta*–by the jaundice; *avidyā*-of ignorance (or in other words, he who is afflicted by the ignorance born of being indifferent to Kṛṣṇa from a time without beginning); *kintu*–but; *khalu*–certainly; *sa eva*–that very sugar-candy of Kṛṣṇa's names, activities and so forth; *juṣṭā*–when taken therapeutically; *anudinam*–constantly; *ādarāt*–with respect or faith; *kramāt*–then gradually; *bhavati*–it becomes; *svādvī*–very tasteful; *hantrī*–and destroys; *mūla*–to the root; *tad-gada*–that disease of indifference to Kṛṣṇa which is expressed in the form of absorption in mundane sense enjoyment

Translation

Aho! Those whose tongues are afflicted by the jaundice of *avidyā* (or, in other words, those who are afflicted by the ignorance born of being indifferent to Śrī Kṛṣṇa from a time without beginning) cannot relish the nectarine names, form, qualities and pastimes of Śrī Kṛṣṇa, which are compared to the sweetest sugar-candy. Instead, these attributes taste bitter to them. But if with great faith one regularly takes this sugar-candy of chanting and hearing the transcendental names, form, qualities and pastimes of Śrī Kṛṣṇa, it gradually becomes relishable to him and destroys at the root his disease, the jaundice of *avidyā* or indifference to Śrī Kṛṣṇa. In other words, he becomes spontaneously attached to Śrī Kṛṣṇa.

Upadeśa-prakāśikā-ṭīkā

When *sādhakas* are still affected by the obstacles which impede progress in devotional life (*anarthas*), their minds are restless and disturbed. For this reason, it is not easy for them to develop a taste for Bhagavān's name and so forth. Still, they should not relent even a little in their determination to continue performing *nāma-bhajana*. Being indifferent to Śrī Kṛṣṇa since beginningless time is called *avidyā*, or ignorance. In this verse such *avidyā* is compared to the disease of jaundice. When one is afflicted with this disease, his tongue's sense of taste is warped. Although Śrī Kṛṣṇa's names, form, qualities and pastimes are like the sweetest sugar-candy, a person afflicted by ignorance does not find them tasteful. By regularly taking sugar-candy, one's jaundice is gradually mitigated and the candy also begins to become tasteful to him. Similarly, by daily cultivating in a regulated manner the limbs of *bhakti*, headed by performing *kīrtana* of Śrī Kṛṣṇa's names and hearing narrations of His pastimes, a *sādhakas' anarthas*, beginning with the tendency to commit offences, are eradicated and natural love for *śrī-nāma* and *hari-kathā* awakens within him.

Pīyūṣa-varṣiṇī-vṛtti

In the third verse of *Śrī Upadeśāmṛta*, qualities and activities which nourish *bhakti* were given. In addition to those qualities and activities, this verse describes the procedure for the cultivation of chanting *kṛṣṇa-nāma* and so forth with *sambandha-jñāna*. The tongue afflicted with the jaundice of *avidyā* cannot narrate Śrī Kṛṣṇa's pastimes or chant His name. But regularly taking the sugar-candy of hearing and chanting Kṛṣṇa's *nāma*, *rūpa*, *guṇa* and *līlā* with great respect is capable of eradicating the disease of ignorance. Each and every *jīva*, like a minute conscious particle within a ray of the complete conscious Kṛṣṇa-sun, is by nature an eternal servant of Śrī Kṛṣṇa. When the *jīva* forgets this fact, he is seized by the disease of ignorance. Due to this, he is devoid of taste for devotional activities, headed by the chanting of Kṛṣṇa's name. But by taking good association and by the resultant mercy received from the *sādhu*, *guru* and Vaiṣṇava, he becomes capable of remembering Kṛṣṇa's names, form, qualities and pastimes and he gradually obtains realisation of his eternal self. As realisation of his eternal nature gradually expands, his taste for devotional activities like chanting *kṛṣṇa-nāma* increases accordingly. Simultaneously his ignorance is dispelled step by step. This is the basis for the comparison to sugar-candy. The tongue of one afflicted with jaundice will not find sugar-candy tasteful. But by taking this candy regularly, his jaundice is gradually cured and that sugar-candy will begin to become tasteful to him. Therefore, with enthusiasm, firm faith and patience, one should always continue to hear and chant Kṛṣṇa's names, form, qualities and pastimes.

Anuvṛtti

Śrī Kṛṣṇa's names, form, qualities and pastimes are compared to sugar-candy, and ignorance is compared to jaundice. Just as delectably sweet sugar-candy does not appeal to the tongue which is afflicted by jaundice, the delightful and delicious sugar-candy of Śrī Kṛṣṇa's names, form, qualities and pastimes does not appeal to the *jīva* who is engulfed by ignorance, due to his indifference to Kṛṣṇa, which has no beginning in time.

If, however, one continuously takes the medicine of this sugar-candy of Śrī Kṛṣṇa's names, form, qualities and pastimes with great honour and faith, the sweet taste of Śrī Kṛṣṇa's name will gradually increase and the disease of material enjoyment, which is rooted in the desire to be aloof from Kṛṣṇa, will be dissipated.

In the *Padma Purāṇa* (*Svarga-khaṇḍa* 48.56), it is confirmed that the principal effect of the holy name will not be immediately experienced when taken by those who are materially engrossed:

tac-cad deha-draviṇa-janatā-lobha-pāṣaṇḍa-madhye
nikṣiptaṁ syān na phala-janakaṁ śīghram evātra vipra

"O *brāhmaṇa*, if the Lord's holy name is cast among the atheists who are lustful towards the body, material possessions and family members, it will not quickly produce the fruit of love for Him."

Due to the influence of ignorance, the *jīva* thinks highly of his material body, family members and material attachments. He mistakenly considers the illusory energy, which is active only where there is an absence of awareness of the Lord, as the supreme controlling entity, Bhagavān. Thus he is unable to understand his true spiritual identity. By the power of Śrī Kṛṣṇa's name, the false egoism arising from the *jīva's* ignorance is dispelled like fog. At that time the *jīva* acquires a taste for performing *kṛṣṇa-bhajana*.

Verse Eight

The Process of Bhajana and the Best Place for Performing Bhajana

तन्नामरूपचरितादि-सुकीर्तनानु-
स्मृत्योः क्रमेण रसनामनसी नियोज्य ।
तिष्ठन् व्रजे तदनुरागिजनानुगामी
कालं नयेदखिलमित्युपदेशसारम् ॥८॥

tan-nāma-rūpa-caritādi-sukīrtanānu-
smṛtyoḥ krameṇa rasanā-manasī niyojya
tiṣṭhan vraje tad-anurāgi-janānugāmī
kālaṁ nayed akhilam ity upadeśa-sāram (8)

Anvaya

tiṣṭhan vraje–living in Vraja; *anugāmī*–as a follower; *anurāgi-jana*–of the eternal residents of Vraja who possess inherent spontaneous love; *tad*–for Him (Śrī Kṛṣṇa); *kālam nayet*–one should utilise all his time; *niyojya*–by engaging; *rasanā*–the tongue; *manasī*–and the mind; *krameṇa*–sequentially; *sukīrtana anu-smṛtyoḥ*–in meticulous chanting and remembrance; *nāma-rūpa-*

caritādi–of the names, form, qualities and pastimes; *tad*–of Him (Vrajendra-nandana Śrī Kṛṣṇa); *iti*–this only; *sāram*–is the essence; *akhilam*–of all; *upadeśa*–instruction

Translation

While living in Vraja as a follower of the eternal residents of Vraja who possess inherent spontaneous love for Śrī Kṛṣṇa, one should utilise all his time by sequentially engaging the tongue and the mind in meticulous chanting and remembrance of Kṛṣṇa's names, form, qualities and pastimes. This is the essence of all instruction.

Upadeśa-prakāśikā-ṭīkā

At this point, these questions may arise in the mind of a new *sādhaka*: "Where should one reside to cultivate the devotional activities, headed by the chanting of Śrī Kṛṣṇa's name, and how should one go about it?" This verse, which constitutes the essence of all instruction, has been composed to answer these questions. The conventional meaning of the name of Kṛṣṇa is drawn from the verbal root *kṛṣ*, which means to attract or draw towards oneself. Thus Kṛṣṇa is famed as the attractor of the hearts of all living entities in the entire world. In Vraja He is known also as Yaśodā-nandana, He who gives delight to Yaśodā. Therefore, all devotees should utilise the entirety of their time in engaging their tongues in performing *kīrtana* of Śrī Kṛṣṇa's name, form, qualities and pastimes and their minds in remembrance of Him. They should reside only in Śrī Vraja-maṇḍala and follow elevated devotees.

How should one follow devotees? By two types of devotion: *vaidhī* (devotion performed in conjunction with the rules and regulations of the scriptures) and *rāgānugā* (spontaneous devotion). Accordingly, there are also two types of *sādhakas*–those who follow the path of *vaidhī* and those who follow the path of *rāgānugā*. Among these two, it is especially desirable to follow a *rāgānugā-bhakta*. The meaning of *tad-anurāgī janānugāmī* is to follow the intimate, eternal devotees in Śrī Kṛṣṇa's *vraja-līlā*. One should cultivate *kṛṣṇa-bhakti* under the guidance of those *rasika gurus* who are themselves followers of the intimate eternal devotees of Śrī Vrajendra-nandana, who enacts human-like pastimes.

Pīyūṣa-varṣiṇī-vṛtti

This verse describes the method of *bhajana* as well as the topmost place for performing *bhajana*. With the intention of incessantly executing the gradual process of *sādhana*, one should utilise every moment of his life by engaging the tongue in nicely performing *kīrtana* of Śrī Kṛṣṇa's names, form, qualities and pastimes and then the mind in *smaraṇa*, or remembrance, upon them. This process should be executed while residing in Vraja and under the guidance of devotees who are immersed in *vraja-rasa*. The performance of this *mānasa-sevā*, or service rendered within the mind, is dependent solely upon residing mentally in Vraja.

Anuvṛtti

By following the rules and regulations prescribed in the previous verses, a *sādhaka* should draw his mind away from everything unrelated to Śrī Kṛṣṇa and engage his tongue in performing *kīrtana* of Kṛṣṇa's *nāma*, *guṇa*, *rūpa* and *līlā*. Then, eventually, his mind will be able to enter into constant remembrance (*smaraṇa*) of Kṛṣṇa. While residing in Vraja, he should utilise all his time executing these activities under the guidance of devotees who are adept at relishing *vraja-rasa*. This is the essence of all instruction.

In the devotional life of a *sādhaka*, *sravaṇa-daśā*, or the stage of hearing, comes first. In this stage, he hears *kṛṣṇa-nāma* and narrations of Kṛṣṇa's qualities, form and pastimes. By doing this more and more, he gradually becomes more mature; then the stage of *varaṇa-daśā* begins. In this stage he begins performing *kīrtana* of those topics he was hearing. By performing *kīrtana* with the specific devotional mood one is cultivating, he enters *smaraṇa-daśā* or the stage of remembrance. Within the category of *smaraṇa* there are five stages: *smaraṇa*, *dhāraṇā*, *dhyāna*, *anusmṛti* and *samādhi*. Meditation where the mind sometimes becomes distracted is called *smaraṇa*. *Smaraṇa* which is devoid of such distraction is called *dhāraṇā*. Unbroken contemplation upon the object of meditation is called *dhyāna*. When *dhyāna* is performed constantly, it is called *anusmṛti*. When one's meditation becomes entirely free from impediments and wholly uninterrupted, it is called *samādhi*. After *smaraṇa-daśā*, one enters the stage known as *āpana-daśā*. In this stage the *sādhaka* achieves realisation of his pure spiritual identity. After this, in the stage known as *sampatti-daśā*, he attains *vastu-siddhi*. At this time, upon shedding the material body, he finally obtains a spiritual form and is appointed to his eternal service in the spiritual realm.

When a devotee following the path of *vaidhī-bhakti* abandons his many varieties of material desires and performs *bhajana* in accordance with the instructions of *śāstra*, *sad-guru* and Vaiṣṇavas, *ruci*, or taste, arises in his *bhajana*. Upon the appearance of this *ruci*, he abandons the path of *vaidhī-bhakti* and enters the path of *rāgānugā-bhakti*.

rāgātmikā-bhakti—'mukhya' vraja-vāsī-jane
tāra anugata-bhaktira 'rāgānugā'-nāme
(*Caitanya-caritāmṛta*, *Madhya-līlā* 22.149)

"That devotion whose very essence is constituted of eternal spontaneous attachment (*rāga*) is known as *rāgātmikā-bhakti*. That devotion is pre-eminent amongst all forms of *bhakti* and is principally manifest in the residents of Vraja. Devotion which follows in the wake of this *rāgātmikā-bhakti* is known as *rāgānugā-bhakti*."

iṣṭe svārasikī rāgaḥ
paramāviṣṭatā bhavet
tanmayī yā bhaved bhaktiḥ
sātra rāgātmikoditā
(*Śrī Bhakti-rasāmṛta-sindhu*, 1.2.272)

"An unquenchable loving thirst (*premamayī-tṛṣṇā*) for the object of one's affection (Śrī Kṛṣṇa) which gives rise to spontaneous and intense absorption (*svārasikī param-āviṣṭatā*) in that object is called *rāga*. Such *rāga-mayī-bhakti*, or the performance of services such as stringing garlands with intense *rāga*, is called *rāgātmikā-bhakti*."

rāgamayī-bhaktira haya 'rāgātmikā' nāma
tāhā śuni' lubdha haya kona bhāgyavān
(*Caitanya-caritāmṛta, Madhya-līlā* 22.152)

"*Bhakti* which consists of *rāga* is called *rāgātmikā*. If, upon hearing of this, a devotee becomes intensely anxious to obtain such devotion, he is considered to be most fortunate."

lobhe vraja-vāsīra bhāve kare anugati
śāstra yukti nāhi mane—rāgānugāra prakṛti
(*Caitanya-caritāmṛta*, *Madhya-līlā* 22.153)

"When one follows in the footsteps of the residents of Vraja (*vraja-vāsīs*) by cultivating their devotional moods with intense hankering, he does not care for the injunctions of the scriptures or for logical arguments. This is the nature of spontaneous devotion."

bāhya, antara—ihāra dui ta' sādhana
'bāhya' sādhaka-dehe kare śravaṇa-kīrtana

'mane' nija-siddha-deha kariyā bhāvana
rātri-dine kare vraje kṛṣṇera sevana
(*Caitanya-caritāmṛta*, *Madhya-līlā* 22.156-157)

"The *sādhana* of *rāgānugā-bhakti* is of two types: external (*bāhya*) and internal (*antara*). Externally one performs hearing and chanting in the *sādhaka-deha*, the outer feature of a practitioner of *bhakti*. Internally, while contemplating one's own perfected spiritual form, one renders service to Śrī Kṛṣṇa in Vraja day and night."

sevā sādhaka-rūpeṇa
siddha-rūpeṇa cātra hi
tad bhāva lipsunā kāryā
vraja-lokānusārataḥ
(*Bhakti-rasāmṛta-sindhu,* 1.2.295)

"A *sādhaka* who has *lobha*, or 'greed', for *rāgānugā-bhakti* should serve Śrī Kṛṣṇa both in the *sādhaka-rūpa* and the *siddha-rūpa* in accordance with the *bhāva* of the eternal devotees residing in Vraja (*vraja-parikaras*) who possess the same mood for which he aspires. The *sādhaka-rūpa* refers to the physical body in which one is presently situated, and the *siddha-rūpa* refers to the internally conceived spiritual form which is suitable to serve Kṛṣṇa according to one's cherished desire."

nijābhīṣṭa kṛṣṇa-preṣṭha pācheta' lāgiyā
nirantara sevā kare antarmanā hañā
(*Caitanya-caritāmṛta, Madhya-līlā* 22.159)

"The eternal residents of Vraja are known as *kṛṣṇa-preṣṭha*, very dear to Śrī Kṛṣṇa. Among Kṛṣṇa's various devotees, those who possess the mood of service towards Him for which one intensely hankers are known as *nijābhīṣṭa kṛṣṇa-preṣṭha*. Following in the footsteps of those beloved devotees of Kṛṣṇa for whose mood of service one hankers, one should constantly serve Kṛṣṇa within the mind through one's internally conceived spiritual form."

kṛṣṇaṁ smaran janaṁ cāsya
preṣṭhaṁ nija-samīhitam
tat-tat-kathā-rataś cāsau
kuryād vāsaṁ vraje sadā
(*Bhakti-rasāmṛta-sindhu*, 1.2.294)

The essential meaning of this verse is that in accordance with one's own specific *bhāva*, the *sādhaka* should remember Śrī Kṛṣṇa and a particular eternal devotee of Kṛṣṇa who possesses the serving mood for which he aspires. He should be immersed in chanting the names of Śrī Kṛṣṇa which are related to His pastimes in Vraja and in hearing narrations of those pastimes. Also, those names and pastimes should be favourable to the *sādhaka's* specific service aspirations. Finally, these activities should be performed while residing in Vraja.

dāsa-sakhā-pitrādi-preyasīra gaṇa
rāga-mārge nija-nija-bhāvera gaṇana
(*Caitanya-caritāmṛta*, *Madhya-līlā* 22.161)

"There are four moods of service which are included in the path of spontaneous devotion: those of the servants, friends, parents and conjugal lovers."

Those desiring to serve in the devotional mellow of neutrality (*śānta-rasa*) should aspire to be like the cows, sticks, buffalo horns, the flute, *kadamba* trees and so forth. Those aspiring to serve in the mellow of servitude (*dāsya-rasa*) should follow servants in Vraja such as Raktaka and Patraka. Devotees aspiring to serve in the mellow of fraternity (*sakhya-rasa*) should follow Śrī Baladeva, Śrīdāmā, Sudāmā and so forth. Devotees aspiring to serve in the mellow of parenthood (*vātsalya-rasa*) should follow Śrī Nanda and Yaśodā, and those aspiring to serve in the conjugal mellow (*mādhurya-rasa*) should follow cowherd girls (*gopīs*) like Lalitā and Viśākhā. While residing in Vraja, one should immerse himself in hearing narrations of the eternal devotees who serve in the mood for which he aspires.

There is no greater place than Vraja-maṇḍala to perform *bhajana* of Śrī Rādhā-Kṛṣṇa. Therefore, even such exalted devotees as Brahmā and Uddhava pray to take birth there as a blade of grass or a shrub.

Verse Nine

What is the Topmost Holy Place?

वैकुण्ठाज्जनितो वरा मधुपुरी तत्रापि रासोत्सवाद्
वृन्दारण्यमुदारपाणिरमणात्तत्रापि गोवर्धनः ।
राधाकुण्डमिहापि गोकुलपतेः प्रेमामृताप्लावनात्
कुर्यादस्य विराजतो गिरितटे सेवां विवेकी न कः ॥९॥

vaikuṇṭhāj janito varā madhu-purī tatrāpi rāsotsavād
vṛndāraṇyam udāra-pāṇi-ramaṇāt tatrāpi govardhanaḥ
rādhā-kuṇḍam ihāpi gokula-pateḥ premāmṛtāplāvanāt
kuryād asya virājato giri-taṭe sevāṁ vivekī na kaḥ (9)

Anvaya

janitaḥ–due to Śrī Kṛṣṇa's having taken birth there; *madhu-purī*–the abode of Mathurā; *varā*–is superior; *vaikuṇṭhāt*–than Vaikuṇṭha, the realm of spiritual opulence; *vṛndāraṇyam*–the forest of Vṛndāvana; (is superior) *tatra api*–even than that (the abode of Mathurā); *rāsa-utsavāt*–because the festival of the rāsa dance took place there; *govardhanaḥ*–Govardhana Hill; (is superior) *tatra api*–even than that (Vṛndāvana forest);

ramaṇāt–because of the playful pastimes (because Śrī Kṛṣṇa raised it with His lotus hand and performed many pastimes there with His devotees); *udāra-pāṇi*–of Śrī Kṛṣṇa, whose hand is mercifully disposed to bestow prema upon His beloved devotees; *rādhā-kuṇḍam*–Śrī Rādhā-kuṇḍa; (is superior) *iha api*–even than this (Govardhana); *āplāvanāt*–due to immersing those (who bathe in its waters); *prema-amṛta*–in the nectar of divine love; *gokula-pateḥ*–of Śrī Kṛṣṇa, the master of Gokula; *kaḥ*–what; *vivekī*–intelligent person; *na kuryāt*–would not render; *sevām*–service; *asya*–to this magnificent pond; *virājitaḥ*–splendidly situated; *taṭe*–at the base; *giri*–of the hill known as Govardhana

Translation

Due to Śrī Kṛṣṇa's having taken birth there, the abode of Mathurā is superior even to Vaikuṇṭha, the realm of spiritual opulence. Superior to Mathurā is the forest of Vṛndāvana because there the festival of the *rāsa* dance took place. Superior to Vṛndāvana forest is Govardhana Hill because Śrī Kṛṣṇa raised it with His lotus hand and performed many pastimes there with His devotees. Yet superior even to Govardhana Hill is

Śrī Rādhā-kuṇḍa because it immerses one in the nectar of Śrī Kṛṣṇa's divine love. What intelligent person would not desire to render service to this magnificent pond, which is splendidly situated at the base of Govardhana Hill?

Upadeśa-prakāśikā-ṭīkā

The previous verse instructed us to perform *bhajana* while residing in Vraja. This verse very clearly answers precisely where one should reside within Vraja. Due to Śrī Kṛṣṇa's having taken birth there, the abode of Mathurā is superior even to Vaikuṇṭha, the realm of great spiritual opulence. Superior even to the abode of Mathurā is the forest of Vṛndāvana because there the festival of the *rāsa* dance took place. Superior to the Vṛndāvana forest is Govardhana Hill because it playfully rested in Śrī Kṛṣṇa's lotus hand, and because there Kṛṣṇa freely enjoyed many pastimes with His devotees. Yet superior even to this Govardhana Hill is the super-excellent Śrī Rādhā-kuṇḍa because it immerses one in the nectarine divine love which Śrī Kṛṣṇa, the moon of Gokula, feels for Śrīmatī Rādhikā. The scriptures declare that Śrī Rādhā-kuṇḍa is as dear to Śrī Kṛṣṇa as the daughter of Vṛṣabhānu Mahārāja, Śrīmatī Rādhikā Herself.

All the above-mentioned spiritual realms or locations where Śrī Kṛṣṇa performed pastimes are manifest from His internal potency (*svarūpa-śakti*) and are therefore purely spiritual. However, Śrī Rādhā-kuṇḍa is superior to them all because of having manifested the highest display of the inherent variegated pastimes of *svarūpa-śakti*.

Pīyūṣa-varṣiṇī vṛtti

This ninth verse informs us that Śrī Rādhā-kuṇḍa is the best amongst all worshipable places. Because Śrī Kṛṣṇa took birth in the city of Mathurā, it is superior to Vaikuṇṭha, the realm of immense opulence in the spiritual sky. Within the district of Mathurā, the Vṛndāvana forest is the best location. Govardhana Hill is the best place within the entire area of Vraja due to Udārapāṇi Śrī Kṛṣṇa having performed various pastimes there. Śrī Rādhā-kuṇḍa is splendidly situated just near Śrī Govardhana. It is the best place of all due to being the special storehouse of Śrī Kṛṣṇa's nectarine divine love (*premāmṛta*). Is there any person intent upon performing *bhajana* who would not desire to render service to Śrī Rādhā-kuṇḍa? In other words, the devotees of Bhagavān most certainly render service to Śrī Rādhā-kuṇḍa. Either in their material bodies or in their spiritually perfected forms, devotees should execute the aforementioned process of *bhajana* while constantly residing at Rādhā-kuṇḍa.

Anuvṛtti

Amongst all holy places, the Vaikuṇṭha realm situated in the spiritual sky is the best. Superior even to Vaikuṇṭha is the district of Mathurā because Bhagavān took birth there. Within Mathurā-maṇḍala, the forest of Vṛndāvana is the best because there the *rāsa* dance took place. Of all places within Vṛndāvana, Govardhana Hill is greater still due to being the site where Śrī Kṛṣṇa freely enjoyed various pastimes. Superior even to Govardhana Hill is Śrī Rādhā-kuṇḍa. Because it overflows with the nectar of Śrī Kṛṣṇa's divine love, it is the best place of all. There is no place greater than Rādhā-kuṇḍa. Therefore, what intelligent person would not render service to Rādhā-kuṇḍa, which is so splendidly situated at the base of Govardhana? In other words, anyone endowed with true spiritual intelligence serves Śrī Rādhā-kuṇḍa.

Śrī Caitanya Mahāprabhu's eternal devotee Śrī Rūpa Gosvāmī, being fully conversant with the most elevated devotional sentiments within Gaurahari's heart, has described service to Śrī Rādhā-kuṇḍa as the topmost. The glories of Śrī Rādhā-kuṇḍa are incomprehensible and inaccessible even for loving devotees who may have taken shelter of *madhura-rasa*, yet are devoid of devotion to Śrī Caitanya Mahāprabhu.

Verse Ten

Who is Śrī Kṛṣṇa's Dearmost Beloved?

कर्मिभ्यः परितो हरेः प्रियतया व्यक्तिंययुर्ज्ञानिन-
स्तेभ्यो ज्ञानविमुक्त-भक्तिपरमाः प्रेमैकनिष्ठास्ततः ।
तेभ्यस्ताः पशुपाल पङ्कजदृशस्ताभ्योऽपि सा राधिका
प्रेष्ठा तद्वदियं तदीयसरसी तां नाश्रयेत् कः कृती ॥१०॥

karmibhyaḥ parito hareḥ priyatayā vyaktiṁ yayur jñāninas
tebhyo jñāna-vimukta-bhakti-paramāḥ premaika-niṣṭhās tataḥ
tebhyas tāḥ paśu-pāla-paṅkaja-dṛśas tābhyo 'pi sā rādhikā
preṣṭhā tadvad iyaṁ tadīya-sarasī tāṁ nāśrayet kaḥ kṛtī (10)

Anvaya

jñāninaḥ–the brahma-jñānīs, who by dint of their spiritual knowledge are transcendental to the three modes of material nature; *yayuḥ*–have attained; *vyaktim*–distinction (have been ascertained in the scriptures; *priyatayā*–as being more dear; *paritaḥ*–in all respects; *hareḥ*–to Śrī Hari; *karmibhyaḥ*–than the pious followers of the path of karma, who are forever occupied in performing virtuous deeds; *jñāna-vimukta*–those who have abandoned the pursuit of knowledge like Sanaka; *bhakti-paramāḥ*–and who are dear devotees of Kṛṣṇa, considering bhakti alone to be the best path; (have attained distinction as being more dear to Śrī Hari) *tebhyaḥ*–than them (the jñanīs); *prema eka-niṣṭhāḥ*–pure devotees of Śrī Kṛṣṇa such as Nārada who are resolutely fixed in prema for Him; (have attained distinction as being more dear to Śrī Hari) *tataḥ*–than them (those dear devotees); *taḥ*–those; *paśu-pāla*–maintainers of the cows (the gopīs); *dṛśaḥ*–whose eyes; *paṅkaja*–are like the fully blossomed petals of a lotus flower; (have attained distinction as being more dear to Śrī Hari) *tebhyaḥ*–than them (those loving devotees); *sā*–that; *rādhikā*–Śrīmatī Rādhikā; (has attained distinction as being more dear to Śrī Hari) *api*–even; *tābhyaḥ*–than them (the gopīs); *iyam*–this; *sarasī*–pond (Śrī Rādhā-kuṇḍa); *tadīya*–of Hers (Śrīmatī Rādhikā); *preṣṭhā*–is more dear (to Śrī Kṛṣṇa); *tad-vat*–just as She is; (therefore) *kaḥ*–what; *kṛtī*–highly fortunate, spiritually intelligent person; *na āśrayet*–would not take shelter (would not reside on the banks of Śrī Rādhā-kuṇḍa in a state of transcendental consciousness, performing bhajana of Śrī Kṛṣṇa's eightfold daily pastimes); *tām*–of that Śrī Rādhā-kuṇḍa

Translation

One who selflessly performs virtuous acts in accordance with the path of *karma-yoga* is superior to those who merely seek to fulfil their selfish desires. The *brahma-jñānīs*, who by dint of their spiritual knowledge are transcendental to the three modes of material nature, are more dear to Śrī Kṛṣṇa than those pious followers of the *karma* path who are forever occupied in performing virtuous deeds. More dear to Śrī Kṛṣṇa than the *brahma-jñānīs* are His devotees like Sanaka, who have abandoned the pursuit of knowledge and who consider *bhakti* alone to be the best path. In doing so, they have followed the statement in *Śrīmad-Bhāgavatam* (10.14.3): *jñāne prayāsam udapāsya*–one should abandon the endeavour for knowledge. Pure devotees like Nārada, who are resolutely fixed in *prema* for Kṛṣṇa, are even more dear to Him than all such devotees. The *vraja-gopīs*, whose very lives belong solely to Kṛṣṇa, are even more beloved to Him than all such loving (*premī*) devotees. Amongst all those beloved *gopīs*, Śrīmatī Rādhikā is more dear to Śrī Kṛṣṇa than His own life; in precisely the same way, He dearly loves Her pond, Śrī Rādhā-kuṇḍa. Therefore, what highly fortunate, spiritually intelligent person would not reside on the banks of Śrī Rādhā-kuṇḍa in a state of transcendental consciousness, performing *bhajana* of Śrī Kṛṣṇa's eightfold daily pastimes?

Upadeśa-prakāśikā-ṭīkā

In this tenth verse, yet another reason for taking shelter of and worshipping Śrī Rādhā-kuṇḍa is being shown. A follower of the path of *karma-kāṇḍa* who is interested solely in enjoying the fruits of his actions is actually indifferent to Bhagavān. More dear to Bhagavān are *jñānīs* who are inclined towards *nirviśeṣa-brahma*, His impersonal aspect, which is merely a nonspecific manifestation of indifferentiated spirit. More dear to Bhagavān than such *jñānīs* are His devotees such as the four Kumāras who are devoid of *nirviśeṣa-jñāna*, inclination towards His impersonal aspect, yet possess *aiśvarya-jñāna*, awareness of His supreme majesty. Devotees such as Śrī Nārada who possess *prema-niṣṭhā*, a resolute and exclusive fixation in love for Him, are even more dear to Śrī Hari than such *jñānī-bhaktas*. Superior to such loving devotees are the *vraja-gopīs* who, due to possessing an indescribable and unprecedented love for Śrī Kṛṣṇa, are exceedingly dear to Him.

In the *Padma Purāṇa* it is said:

yathā rādhā priyā viṣṇos
tasyāḥ kuṇḍaṁ priyaṁ tathā
sarva-gopīṣu saivaikā
viṣṇor atyanta-vallabhā

"Just as Śrīmatī Rādhikā is most dear to Śrī Kṛṣṇa, Her pond, Śrī Rādhā-kuṇḍa, is equally dear to Him. Among all the beloved *gopīs*, none are as dear as Śrīmatī Rādhikā."

This verse, quoted in *Ujjvala-nīlamaṇi* (4.5), proves that, amongst all the *gopīs*, Śrīmatī Rādhikā alone is Śrī Kṛṣṇa's dearmost beloved. In precisely the same way, Śrī Rādhā-kuṇḍa, Her pond which is actually nondifferent from Her, is exceedingly dear to Śrī Kṛṣṇa and is also the topmost place of residence for devotees. Therefore, what spiritually insightful person desirous of performing *bhajana* would not take shelter of that pond? Certainly any such person would take shelter of Śrī Rādhā-kuṇḍa.

Pīyūṣa-varṣiṇī-vṛtti

Among the many varieties of *sādhakas* found in this world, the devotee of Bhagavān who performs *bhajana* while residing on the banks of Śrī Rādhā-kuṇḍa is the best and the most dear to Śrī Kṛṣṇa. This is described in this tenth verse. More dear to Kṛṣṇa than the followers of the path of *karma* are the *jñānīs* who search after the impersonal aspect of the absolute truth. More dear to Kṛṣṇa than all the varieties of *jñānīs* is a pure devotee who has abandoned the attempt to understand the absolute truth through the cultivation of knowledge. Amongst all varieties of pure devotees, the *premī-bhakta*, or one who dearly loves Kṛṣṇa, is the most dear to Him. Amongst all varieties of such loving pure devotees, the *vraja-gopīs* are the most dear to Kṛṣṇa. Of all the *vraja-gopīs*, Śrīmatī Rādhikā is Kṛṣṇa's dearmost, and Her pond, Śrī Rādhā-kuṇḍa, is similarly dear to Him. Therefore, the intelligent person who possesses sufficient accumulated devotional merit (*sukṛti*) will most certainly reside on the banks of Śrī Rādhā-kuṇḍa and within the mind render service to Śrī Kṛṣṇa's eightfold daily pastimes.

Anuvṛtti

More dear to Śrī Kṛṣṇa than those who simply act to fulfil their selfish desires is one who is firmly established in the mode of goodness and is therefore dedicated to performing virtuous deeds. Even more dear to Kṛṣṇa than all such *sat-karmīs* is a *brahma-jñānī* who is transcendental to the modes of nature altogether. More dear to Kṛṣṇa than all such *jñānīs* is a pure devotee. More dear to Kṛṣṇa than all such pure devotees is a *premī-bhakta* who loves Him dearly. Even more dear to Kṛṣṇa than all such *premī-bhaktas* are the *vraja-gopīs*. Amongst all the *vraja-gopīs*, Śrīmatī Rādhikā is Kṛṣṇa's dearmost. In the same way that Kṛṣṇa loves Her, He loves Her pond, Śrī Rādhā-kuṇḍa. Therefore, Kṛṣṇa's devotees, who are the most fortunate people, take shelter of Śrī Rādhā-kuṇḍa.

Verse Eleven

The Glories of Śrī Rādhā-kuṇḍa

कृष्णस्योच्चैः प्रणयवसतिःप्रेयसीभ्योऽपिराधा-
कुण्डं चास्या मुनिभिरभितस्तदृगेव व्यधायि ।
यत् प्रेष्ठैरप्यलमसुलभं किं पुनर्भक्तिभाजां
तत्प्रेमेदं सकृदपिसरः स्नातुराविष्करोति ॥११॥

kṛṣṇasyoccaiḥ praṇaya-vasatiḥ preyasībhyo 'pi rādhā
kuṇḍaṁ cāsyā munibhir abhitas tādṛg eva vyadhāyi
yat preṣṭhair apy alam asulabhaṁ kiṁ punar bhakti-bhājāṁ
tat premedaṁ sakṛd api saraḥ snātur āviṣkaroti (11)

Anvaya

rādhā–Śrīmatī Rādhikā; *preyasībhyaḥ api*–even more than the other beloved gopīs; *uccaiḥ*–is the foremost; *vasati*–object; *praṇaya*-of love; *kṛṣṇasya*–of Śrī Kṛṣṇa; *asyāḥ*–Her (Śrīmatī Rādhikā's); *kuṇḍam*–pond; *ca*–also; *abhitaḥ*–in every respect; *tādṛk eva*–is just so (the topmost object of Śrī Kṛṣṇa's love); *vyadhāyi*–this has been established (in the scriptures); *munibhiḥ*–by the sages; *idam*–this; *saraḥ*–pond (Śrī Rādhā-kuṇḍa);

āviṣkaroti–bestows; *tat*–that; *prema*–gopī-prema; *yat*–which; *alam*–is immensely; *asulabham*–difficult to attain; *preṣṭhaiḥ api*–even for such dear devotees of Bhagavān as Nārada; *kim punar*–what to speak of; *bhakti bhājām*–other reservoirs of bhakti (the sādhaka-bhaktas); *snātuḥ*–upon one who simply bathes in its waters with great devotion; *sakṛt api*–only once

Translation

After thorough deliberation on the matter, the sages have unanimously declared (in the *Padma Purāṇa*) that just as amongst all the *gopīs* Śrīmatī Rādhikā is the foremost object of Śrī Kṛṣṇa's great love, in precisely the same way this pond of Hers is also the topmost object of His love. Upon one who simply bathes in its waters just once with great devotion, Śrī Rādhā-kuṇḍa bestows that rare treasure of *gopī-prema* which is so immensely difficult to attain even for such dear devotees of Bhagavān as Nārada–what to speak of ordinary *sādhakas*.

Upadeśa-prakāśikā-ṭīkā

It is only natural at this point to become eager to learn what special commodity can be attained by taking exclusive shelter of the limitlessly glorious Śrī Rādhā-kuṇḍa. "The fruit of such exclusive devotion is the topmost variety of *kṛṣṇa-prema*"–Śrī Rūpa Gosvāmī is concluding his composition by affirming this philosophical principle (*siddhānta*). The *prema* being spoken of here is extremely difficult to achieve even for such exalted and dear devotees of Bhagavān as Nārada. In other words, this most elevated, radiant divine love *(unnatojjvala-prema)* which the *vraja-gopīs* possess for Śrī Kṛṣṇa is not only difficult for such dear devotees to attain, it is actually impossible. Śrī Rādhā-kuṇḍa bestows this very *prema* upon one who bathes in its waters with a mood of special love and devotion. Here, Śrī Rādhā-kuṇḍa is both the *svayaṁ-karttā*, or the one who directly bestows that *prema* upon the devotees, and also the *viṣaya*, or object of the devotees' love. Who would not take shelter of this Rādhā-kuṇḍa? In other words, any devotee, skilled in the art of performing *bhajana* and sincerely desirous of achieving the topmost *prema*, would certainly do so.

Relying upon a particle of Śrī Caitanya Mahāprabhu's mercy, I have composed this commentary as far as my intelligence allows in order to increase the transcendental pleasure of His devotees. This servant of the Śrī Rādhā-ramaṇa Deity and son of Śrī Govardhana-lāla, named Rādhā-ramaṇa dāsa, hereby concludes his commentary named *Upadeśa-prakāśikā* on Śrī Rūpa Gosvāmī's *Śrī Upadeśāmṛta.*

Pīyūṣa-varṣiṇī-vṛtti

Having described the natural glory of Śrī Rādhā-kuṇḍa in the previous verse, this eleventh verse has been composed with the intention of making steadfast faith in Śrī Rādhā-kuṇḍa arise within the hearts of *sādhakas.* Śrīmatī Rādhikā is Śrī Kṛṣṇa's dearmost beloved and in all respects more exalted than all His other beloveds. In the scriptures, the sages (*munis*) have described Śrī Rādhā-kuṇḍa's eminence in the same way. Śrī Rādhā-kuṇḍa easily bestows upon one who bathes in its waters that rare *prema* which is not only immensely difficult for *sādhakas* to attain, but also difficult for *premī-bhaktas* like Nārada to achieve.

Therefore, Śrī Rādhā-kuṇḍa alone is the most suitable place of residence for those endeavouring for perfection in their *bhajana*. The *jīva* who has overcome the influence of matter and who has attained his inner perfected spiritual form as a *gopī* (*aprākṛta-gopī-deha*) should reside, in the mood of a maidservant (*pālyadāsī*) of Śrīmatī Rādhikā, on the banks of transcendental Śrī Rādhā-kuṇḍa in the divine land of Vraja (*aprākṛta-vraja*) in the resplendent grove (*kuñja*) of the spiritual master, who is situated in his eternal form as a female friend (*guru-rūpā-sakhī*) of Śrī Rādhā-Kṛṣṇa. Living there, the pure spirit soul (*aprākṛta-jīva*) should externally take constant shelter of chanting *harināma*. Internally, in his spiritually perfected eternal form as a *gopī*, he should render service to Śrīmatī Rādhikā while deeply meditating on Śrī Kṛṣṇa's eightfold daily pastimes (*aṣṭa-kālīya-līlā*). This is the culmination of *bhajana* for the devotees who have taken shelter of Śrī Caitanya Mahāprabhu's feet.

Anuvṛtti

Śrīmatī Rādhikā is Śrī Kṛṣṇa's dearmost beloved and the crest-jewel of those who are dear to Him. In the scriptures, devotee sages have described Śrī Rādhā-kuṇḍa as being Śrī Kṛṣṇa's foremost beloved object, as dear to Him as Śrīmatī Rādhikā Herself. The topmost love for Bhagavān, *gopī-prema*, is exceedingly difficult even for dearly beloved devotees of Bhagavān such as Nārada to attain. So what to speak of how difficult it is for devotees still in the practitioner stage (*sādhaka-bhaktas*) to achieve that rare *prema*! But very easily Śrī Rādhā-kuṇḍa bestows this *prema* upon one who bathes in its waters just once.

Śrī Rādhā-kuṇḍa is full of *prema* and, indeed, is actually comprised of waters of nectarine *prema*. By transcendentally residing (*aprākṛta-vāsa*) on the banks of Śrī Rādhā-kuṇḍa and by transcendentally bathing (*aprākṛta-snāna*) in its waters, one will obtain the topmost *prema*. What is meant by *aprākṛta-vāsa* and *aprākṛta-snāna*? Remaining thoroughly aloof from all desires for material sense enjoyment, one should constantly perform deep meditational worship (*mānasa-bhajana*) in strict devotion to Śrīmatī Rādhikā for the duration of one's life. After shedding this material body, one will attain an eternal spiritual body and be intently engaged in direct, eternal service to Śrīmatī Rādhikā. Only one who bathes in Śrī Rādhā-kuṇḍa in this way attains the topmost *prema*.

Obtaining such good fortune is exceedingly difficult even for such exalted *premī* devotees as Nārada. It is extremely difficult even for the perfected devotees who eternally serve Kṛṣṇa in the devotional mellows (*rasas*) of servitude (*dāsya*), friendship (*sakhya*) and parenthood (*vātsalya*) to bathe in Śrī Rādhā-kuṇḍa, what to speak of worldly-minded persons. What more can possibly be said of the glories of taking *aprākṛta-snāna* in Śrī Rādhā-kuṇḍa? Those who bathe there obtain good fortune which extends all the way up to becoming maidservants of Śrī Vārṣabhānavī (Śrīmatī Rādhikā).

Śrī Govinda dāsa was Śrī Caitanya Mahāprabhu's dear servant. Always accompanying Mahāprabhu as if he were His shadow, he served Mahāprabhu with great love. Simultaneously he would also record in his own words descriptions of Śrīman Mahāprabhu's especially significant pastimes. The collection of verses he wrote became famous by the name of *Govinda-kaḍacā*. Having heard these verses directly from Śrī Raghunātha dāsa Gosvāmī,

Śrī Kṛṣṇadāsa Kavirāja Gosvāmī explained them in his own words in his *Śrī Caitanya-caritāmṛta*. Through the medium of those verses, light was shed upon Śrī Caitanya Mahāprabhu's transcendental character.

The following is a narration from the time when Śrīman Mahāprabhu was residing in Jagannātha Purī: Mahāprabhu had already fulfilled the objectives for which He descended upon this Earth. Now He desired to wind up His pastimes. One day He took His intimate devotees and went to the shore of the ocean. Seeing the blue ocean, remembrance of Śyāmasundara immediately arose within Him. Becoming overwhelmed in devotional ecstacy (*bhāva*), He was oblivious to all else. With great difficulty His devotees gradually brought Him back to external consciousness. At that very time Śrī Gaurasundara slowly began instructing those devotees. In that assembly of devotees, Mahāprabhu's very dear disciple Śrī Rūpa Gosvāmī was also present. Rūpa Gosvāmī wrote those instructions down in verse form. These verses became famous as *Śrī Upadeśāmṛta*, nectarine instructions. For spiritual practitioners, this *Upadeśāmṛta* is like their very lives and a necklace to be worn at all times.

A servant of the famous Śrī Rādhā-ramaṇa Deity in Vṛndāvana, named Śrī Rādhā-ramaṇa dāsa Gosvāmī, composed a beautiful commentary entitled *Upadeśa-prakāśikā-ṭīkā* on the eleven verses of *Śrī Upadeśāmṛta*. After some time, the condition of the residents of this world became critical, due to the doctrine of *prema-bhakti* having been substantially covered by the frightful influence of the present age of Kali-yuga. Seeing this, Śrī Caitanya Mahāprabhu sent His dear, eternal devotee Śrī Bhaktivinoda Ṭhākura to this world. In simple and comprehensible language, he composed a brief yet essential commentary on the verses of *Śrī Upadeśāmṛta*. This commentary is famous as *Pīyūṣa-varṣiṇī-vṛtti*.

Śrī Gaurasundara is the personification of *aprākṛta vipralambha-rasa*, the mellow constituted of sentiments of divine separation from Śrī Kṛṣṇa. To nourish the *rasa* of *sambhoga*, which is when the devotee is meeting together with Kṛṣṇa, He tasted that *vipralambha-rasa*, and for the benefit of human society He taught how it can be attained. It is compulsory for sincere *sādhakas* to accept these instructions. Otherwise, it will be impossible for them to ever achieve *kṛṣṇa-prema*.

In modern times, Kali Mahārāja, the personification of the present degraded age, has assumed the bogus dress of a devotee of Śrī Gaura. Sometimes he adopts the name of *sahajiyā* or imitationist cults such as Āula, Bāula, Neḍā or Neḍī. With great intensity he propagates these false philosophies, as well as other doctrines such as *māyāvāda* and *gaura-nāgarī*,[8] which are opposed to the path of *bhakti*. Aho! Just see the influence of Kali Mahārāja! Some say, "I am Gaurahari Himself," some declare themselves to be glorious spiritual masters, some consider themselves to be the Creator, and others say that they are Śiva. Very enthusiastically they cheat human society by propagating their bogus philosophies

[8] In the transcendental loving affairs of Śrī Rādhā-Kṛṣṇa, Śrī Kṛṣṇa is *nāgara*, the predominating hero in the position of the enjoyer, and Śrī Rādhā and Her bodily manifestations, the *sakhīs*, are *nāgarīs*, the predominated heroines in the position of the enjoyed. Although Śrī Gaura is Kṛṣṇa Himself, He adopts the mood of the *nāgarī*, Śrīmatī Rādhikā, in order to experience the nature of Her love for Kṛṣṇa. Therefore, Śrī Gaurāṅga is not in the mood of a *nāgara*. The *gaura-nāgarīs* conceive of Śrīman Mahāprabhu as a *nāgara* and themselves as *nāgarīs*. This is completely opposed to both the mood of Mahāprabhu and the cultivation of *śuddha-bhakti*.

which they were taught by Kali Mahārāja. Being pleased with their preaching, Kali Mahārāja blesses them and bestows upon them abundant wealth (*kanaka*), women (*kāminī*) and notoriety (*pratiṣṭhā*). Being bewildered by their propaganda, most people ignore *śuddha-bhakti* and *bhagavat-bhajana* and instead advance along the path of these new, depraved philosophies which are based on material enjoyment. They become so intoxicated in this mundane enjoyment that they are completely unaware of just how they are ascending the peak of thorough self-destruction.

O faithful devotees! Don't move in that direction. Become steadfastly situated upon the path of *bhakti* which was shown by great personalities such as Śrī Svarūpa Dāmodara, Śrī Rūpa Gosvāmī, Śrī Raghunātha dāsa Gosvāmī, and Śrī Narottama Ṭhākura. This devotional path enables one to relish the pure *kṛṣṇa-prema* which was practiced and preached by Śrī Gaura-Nityānanda. Reside in Vraja and always perform *kīrtana* and *smaraṇa* of Śrī Rādhā-Kṛṣṇa's *nāma*, *rūpa*, *guṇa* and *līlā*. The doctrine of *gaura-nāgarī* is a bogus philosophy which is opposed to *bhakti*. Remain aloof from such bogus philosophies. The embodiments of *prema-bhakti*, Śrī Viṣṇupriya and Śrī Lakṣmīpriya, as well as the embodiment of the holy *dhāma*, Śrī Nīlādevī, perpetually serve Śrī Gaurasundara, who is the combined form of Śrī Rādhā-Kṛṣṇa. Knowing this to be true, take shelter of Him and, following in the footsteps of the *vraja-gopīs*, day and night render devotional service within the mind. By doing so, even that *prema-sevā* of Śrī Rādhā-Kṛṣṇa which is extremely difficult to obtain will become easily attainable.

Śrī Bhaktivinoda Ṭhākura revealed the holy *dhāma* of Māyāpura. There he established the regular worship of Deities, including Śrī Gaura-Nityānanda, Śrī Gaura-Gadādhara, Śrī Gaura-Viṣṇupriya and Śrī Gaura-Lakṣmīpriya. Everywhere he preached the holy names of Śrī Gaura and Śrī Kṛṣṇa as well as the doctrine of *śuddha-bhakti*. Besides composing many of his own books on *śuddha-bhakti*, he translated many ancient devotional scriptures and wrote numerous commentaries, essays and articles.

Towards the end of his life, upon seeing the dearth of *bhakti* in society, he deprived the people by ceasing his attempts to deliver them. On the pretext of old age, he adopted a vow of silence and remained immersed in *mānasī-sevā*, devotional service performed within meditation. Overwhelmed with compassion for the souls suffering in this world, with tearful eyes he looked towards me and ordered me to preach the doctrine of *śuddha-bhakti* that was revealed by Śrī Caitanya Mahāprabhu and His eternal devotees. He also instructed me to compose this *Anuvṛtti* commentary illuminating his *Pīyūṣa-varṣiṇī-vṛtti* commentary on *Śrī Upadeśāmṛta*. Taking the dust of his divine feet upon my head, I have followed his command. But just when I had completed commenting on eight verses of *Śrī Upadeśāmṛta*, he departed this world from Svānanda-sukhada-kuñja at Śrī Rādhā-kuṇḍa and entered into Śrī Rādhā-Kṛṣṇa's eternal pastimes.

O Śrī Bhaktivinoda Ṭhākura, intimate devotee of Śrīmatī Rādhikā! On this day of completing my *Anuvṛtti* commentary on the verses of *Śrī Upadeśāmṛta*, this destitute servant of yours offers it into your lotus hands. May you be pleased. All glories unto you!

Remembering Śrī Gauracandra, on this twenty-second day of the lunar month of Bhādrapada in the year 1914 at Candraśekhara-bhavana in Māyāpura, I have completed this *Anuvṛtti* commentary.

Glossary

A

Abhidheya–the means by which the ultimate goal is achieved; the practices of devotional life.

Ācārya–spiritual preceptor; one who teaches by example.

Anarthas–unwanted desires in the heart which impede one's advancement in devotional life. These *anarthas* are of four types: (1) *duṣkṛtottha*–those arising from past sins, (2) *sukṛtottha*–those arising from previous pious activities, (3) *aparādhottha*–those arising from offenses, and (4) *bhaktyuttha*–those arising in relationship to one's devotion (*bhakti*).

Aṅgas–(1) limbs, divisions, parts; (2) the various practices of devotional life such as hearing and chanting are referred to as *aṅgas*.

Aparādhī–one who commits *aparādha*, or offences, against the holy name, the Vaiṣṇavas, the *guru*, the scriptures, the holy places, the Deity and so on. The word *rādha* means to give pleasure, and the word *apa* means taking away. Thus the word *aparādha* signifies all activities that are displeasing to the Lord and His devotees. One who commits such *aparādha* is known as an *aparādhī*.

Āsakti–attachment. This especially refers to attachment for the Lord and His eternal devotees. *Āsakti* occurs when one's affection for the process of worshipping the Lord leads to a direct and deep attachment for Him. This is the sixth stage in the development of the creeper of devotion and it is awakened upon the maturing of one's taste (*ruci*) for *bhajana*.

Aṣṭa-kālīya-līlā–the pastimes which Śrī Kṛṣṇa performs with His devotees in eight periods of the day. Practitioners of devotional life who are engaged in *smaraṇa*, or remembrance, meditate on these pastimes. The periods are as follows (times are approximate): (1) *niśānta-līlā*–pastimes at the end of night (3:36 am-6:00 am), (2) *prātaḥ-līlā*–pastimes at dawn (6:00 am-8:24 am), (3) *pūrvāhna-līlā*–morning pastimes (8:24 am-10:48 am), (4) *madhyāhna-līlā*–midday pastimes (10:48 am-3:36 pm), (5) *aparāhna-līlā*–afternoon pastimes (3:36 pm-6:00 pm), (6) *sāyāhna-līlā*–pastimes at dusk (6:00 pm-8:24 pm), (7) *pradoṣa-līlā*–evening pastimes (8:24 pm-10:48 pm), and (8) *nakta-līlā*–midnight pastimes (10:48 pm-3:36 am).

Avadhūta–an ascetic who often transgresses the rules governing ordinary social conduct.

B

Bhagavān–the Supreme Lord who possesses in full the six fortunes of opulence, religiosity, fame, beauty, knowledge and renunciation.

Bhagavat-anuśīlana–the word *anuśīlana* refers to constant practice, study or cultivation. When it is performed in relation to devotion to the Lord, it is known as *bhagavat-anuśīlana*.

Bhagavat-prema–love for Śrī Kṛṣṇa which is extremely concentrated, which completely melts the heart, and which gives rise to a deep sense of possessiveness in relationship to Him.

Bhajana–(1) the word *bhajana* is derived from the verbal root *bhaj* which is defined as follows in the *Garuḍa Purāṇa* (*Pūrva-khaṇḍa* 231.3): "The verbal root *bhaj* is used specifically in the sense of service (*sevā*). Therefore, when devotional practices are performed with the consciousness of being a servant, it is called *bhakti*." According to this verse, loving devotional service to Śrī Kṛṣṇa is called *bhakti*. Such service is the intrinsic attribute of *bhakti* or *bhajana*. Therefore, whatever services are performed in this consciousness may be referred to as *bhajana*; (2) in the general sense *bhajana* refers to spiritual practices, especially hearing, chanting, and meditating upon the holy name, form, qualities and pastimes of Śrī Kṛṣṇa.

Bhajana-mālā–a rosary of beads made from the wood of the sacred *tulasī* plant which devotees of Śrī Kṛṣṇa use for private chanting of the *hare kṛṣṇa mantra.*

Bhakti–the word *bhakti* comes from the root *bhaj*, which means to serve (see *bhajana*). Therefore, the primary meaning of the word *bhakti* is to render service. The performance of activities which are meant exclusively for the pleasure of Śrī Kṛṣṇa, which are done in a favourable spirit saturated with love, which are devoid of all other desires, and which are not covered by the pursuits of fruitive activity (*karma*) and the cultivation of knowledge aimed at merging one's existence into that of the Lord (*jñāna*) is called *bhakti.*

Bhakti-tattva–the word *tattva* refers to a truth, a reality, or a philosophical principle. Those related to devotional life are known as *bhakti-tattva.*

Bhāva–spiritual emotions, love, sentiment.

Bhāva-bhakti–the initial stage of perfection in devotion. A stage of *bhakti* in which the essence of the Lord's internal potency consisting of spiritual knowledge and bliss (*viśuddha-sattva*) is transmitted into the heart of the practicing devotee from the heart of the

Lord's eternal associates. It then softens the heart by different kinds of taste. *Bhāva-bhakti* is the first sprout of pure love of God (*prema*).

Brahma–the impersonal, all-pervading feature of the Lord, which is devoid of attributes and qualities. It is also sometimes known as Brahman.

Brāhmaṇa–the intellectual class amongst the four castes (*varṇas*) within the Vedic social system (*varṇāśrama*).

D

Dāsya-rasa–one of the five primary relationships with Śrī Kṛṣṇa which is established within the devotee's heart in the perfectional stage of *bhāva* or *prema*. In this relationship, the devotee's love for the Lord is expressed in the mood of a servant.

Devatās–demigods situated in the heavenly planets who are entrusted with specific powers for the purpose of universal administration.

Dīkṣā-guru–the initiating spiritual master. One who gives a *mantra* in accordance with the regulations of scripture to a qualified candidate for the purpose of worshipping the Lord and realising Him through that *mantra* is known as a *dīkṣā-guru* or *mantra-guru*,

G

Gaura-nāgarī–in the transcendental loving affairs of Śrī Rādhā-Kṛṣṇa, Śrī Kṛṣṇa is *nāgara*, the predominating hero in the position of the enjoyer, and Śrī Rādhā as well as Her bodily manifestations, the *sakhīs*, are *nāgarīs*, the predominated heroines in the position of the enjoyed. Although Śrī Gaura is Kṛṣṇa Himself, He adopts the mood of the *nāgarī*, Śrīmatī Rādhikā, in order to experience the nature of Her love for Kṛṣṇa. Therefore, Śrī Gaurāṅga is not in the mood of a *nāgara*. The *gaura-nāgarīs* conceive of Śrīman Mahāprabhu as a *nāgara* and themselves as *nāgarīs*. This is completely opposed to both the mood of Mahāprabhu and the cultivation of *śuddha-bhakti*.

Gṛhastha–household life, and the second stage of life (*āśrama*) within the Vedic social system (*varṇāśrama*).

Gosvāmī–one who is the master of his senses; a title for those in the renounced order of life.

Gopīs–the young cowherd maidens of Vraja, headed by Śrīmatī Rādhikā, who serve Śrī Kṛṣṇa in the mood of amorous love. This may also refer to the elderly *gopīs*, headed by mother Yaśodā, who serve Kṛṣṇa in the mood of parental affection.

Go-dāsa–one who is enslaved by the urges of the material senses.

Guṇa–Śrī Kṛṣṇa's transcendental qualities which are heard, described and meditated upon by devotees as part of their devotional practice.

Guru-rūpā-sakhī–the spiritual master in his eternal spiritual form as a female maidservant of Śrī Rādhā-Kṛṣṇa.

J

Jīvas–the eternal, individual living entity who in the conditioned state of material existence assumes a material body in any of the innumerable species of life.

Jñāna–(1) knowledge; (2) the pursuit of knowledge with the intention of merging the soul's individual identity with the impersonal aspect of the Lord.

K

Kāma–(1) lust to gratify the urges of the material senses; (2) the *gopīs*' transcendental desire to enjoy amorous pastimes with Śrī Kṛṣṇa.

Kaniṣṭha-adhikārī–the neophyte practitioner of devotional life.

Karma–(1) any activity performed in the course of material existence; (2) reward-seeking activities; pious activities leading to material gain in this world or in the heavenly planets after death; (3) fate; previous actions which yield inevitable reactions.

Kṛṣṇa-kathā–narrations of the holy names, form, qualities and pastimes of Śrī Kṛṣṇa.

Kuṇḍa–a pond or lake.

Kuñja–a grove or bower; a natural shady retreat, the sides and roof of which are formed mainly by trees and climbing plants.

L

Līlā–divine sportive pastimes. The Lord's activities, whether in the matter of the creation of the material world or in the matter of transcendental exchanges of love with His devotees, are never under the influence of material nature. They are all manifestations of His self-willed potencies and therefore they are known as *līlā*, or divine sport. These pastimes are heard, described and meditated upon by devotees as part of their devotional practice.

M

Mādhurya-rasa–the topmost of the five primary relationships with Śrī Kṛṣṇa which is established within the devotee's heart in the perfectional stage of *bhāva* or *prema*. In this relationship, the devotee's love for the Lord is expressed in the mood of a lover.

Madhyama-adhikārī–the practitioner of devotional life who has reached the intermediate stage of spiritual development.

Mahābhāva–the highest stage of divine love.

Mahājanas–great personalities who teach the highest ideal and who by their conduct set an example for others to follow.

Mahā-prasāda–the remnants of food offered to the Deity; it may also refer to the remnants of other articles offered to the Deity such as incense, flowers, garlands and clothing.

Mānasa-sevā–service rendered within the mind to one's worshipable Deity.

Maṭha–a monastery or temple.

Māyāvāda–the doctrine of illusion; a theory advocated by the impersonalist followers of Śaṅkarācārya which holds that the Lord's form, this material world and the individual existence of the living entities is *māyā*, or false.

Muni–a sage, ascetic or spiritual scholar.

N

Nāma–the holy name of the Lord, which is chanted by devotees as part of their devotional practice.

Nāmāparādha–offenses against the holy name, of which there are ten varieties.

Nirviśeṣa-vādīs–those who advocate the doctrine that ultimately the Lord is devoid of personal qualities and that merging into the indifferentiated *brahma* is the ultimate spiritual perfection of the living entity.

Niskiñcana–the state of having renounced all one's material possessions.

Niṣṭhā–firm faith which results in steadiness in one's devotional practices. This is the fourth stage in the development of the devotional creeper. It occurs after the elimination of a significant portion of one's *anarthas*.

P

Pālyadāsī–a maidservant of Śrīmatī Rādhikā. The word *pālya* means to be nourished, cared for and protected, and the word *dāsī* means a female servant. Thus the *pālyadāsīs* are maidservants under the affectionate care of Śrīmatī Rādhikā.

Paramahaṁsa–the topmost, swan-like devotee.

Praṇāma–an obeisance.

Prāṇanātha–literally means the Lord of one's life, but it has the sense of one who is infinitely more dear than life itself.

Prayojana–the ultimate goal of devotional life, unadulterated love for Śrī Kṛṣṇa.

Prema-bhakti–a stage of devotion which is characterised by the appearance of divine love (*prema*); the perfectional stage of devotion. This is the eighth and final stage in the development of the devotional creeper.

Premamayī–saturated with divine love.

Prema-dharma–the religion of divine love as propagated and practiced by Śrī Caitanya Mahāprabhu.

Prema-avatāra–the incarnation of love, Śrī Caitanya Mahāprabhu.

R

Rāga-mārga–the path of spontaneous attachment (*rāga*).

Rāgānugā-bhakti–an elevated stage of devotion which is motivated by spontaneous attraction or love.

Rāgātmikā-bhakti–the spontaneous devotion which resides exclusively within the hearts of Śrī Kṛṣṇa's eternal devotees in the spiritual world.

Rasika–one who relishes the mellows of devotion (*rasa*) within his heart.

Ruci–taste. The awakening of taste for hearing, chanting and other such devotional practices means that one has greater liking for these activities than any type of material activity. At this stage, one's attraction to spiritual matters exceeds one's attraction to material things. This is the fifth stage in the development of the devotional creeper. It occurs after one has acquired steadiness in his devotional practice.

Rūpa–form, shape, appearance; when used in relationship with Śrī Kṛṣṇa, this refers to His transcendental eternal form which is heard about, described and meditated upon by devotees as part of their devotional practice.

S

Sad-guru–a perfected spiritual master.

Sādhaka–one who follows a spiritual discipline with the objective of achieving pure devotion for Śrī Kṛṣṇa.

Sādhana-bhakti–the stage of devotional life in which a spiritual discipline is performed for the purpose of bringing about the manifestation of *bhāva*, or ecstatic, pure love for Śrī Kṛṣṇa.

Sādhu-saṅga–the association of highly advanced devotees who possess pure devotion for Śrī Kṛṣṇa. This is the first development of the devotional creeper after its initial inception in the form of faith (*śraddhā*).

Sahajiyā–one who considers the stages of advanced devotion to be easily achieved and who thus sometimes imitates the external symptoms of spiritual ecstacy associated with those stages.

Sakhya-rasa–one of the five primary relationships with Śrī Kṛṣṇa which is established within the devotee's heart in the perfectional stage of *bhāva* or *prema*. In this relationship, the devotee's love for the Lord is expressed in the mood of a friend.

Sambandha–the principle regarding the mutual relationships between the Lord, the living entities and the material energy.

Sambandha-jñāna–knowledge regarding *sambandha-tattva*, the mutual relationship between the Lord, the living entities and the material energy. The word *sambandha* means connection, relationship and binding. The living entities are eternally and inseparably connected to the Supreme Lord. Therefore, He is the true object of relationship. The general relationship between the living entities and the Supreme Lord is one of servant and served. However, in the perfectional stage of devotion one becomes established in a specific relationship with the Lord either as a servant, friend, parent or lover.

Sampradāya–a school of religious thought.

Sannyāsa–renounced ascetic life, and the fourth stage of life (*āśrama*) within the Vedic social system (*varṇāśrama*).

Śānta-rasa–the first of the five primary relationships with Śrī Kṛṣṇa which is established within the devotee's heart in the perfectional stage of *bhāva* or *prema*. In this devotional mellow (*rasa*), the devotee's love for the Lord is expressed in a mood of neutrality.

Śaraṇāgati–full surrender to Śrī Kṛṣṇa or His representative, the spiritual master.

Śāstra–the revealed scriptures.

Siddha-bhakta–a devotee who has achieved spiritual perfection. *Siddha-bhaktas* are described in *Bhakti-rasāmṛta-sindhu* (2.1.180): "One who is always fully immersed in activities related to Śrī Kṛṣṇa, who is completely unacquainted with material distress, and who incessantly tastes the bliss of divine love (*prema*) is called a *siddha-bhakta*."

Siddhānta–a philosophical doctrine or precept, a demonstrated conclusion, an established end, or an admitted truth.

Śikṣā-guru–the person from whom one receives instructions about how to progress on the devotional path is known as the *śikṣā-guru*, or instructing spiritual master.

Smaraṇa–remembrance and meditation upon Śrī Kṛṣṇa's names, form, qualities and pastimes.

Śraddhā–faith. This refers to faith in the statements of the scriptures which is awakened after accumulating pious merit through the performance of devotional activities over many births. Such faith is aroused in the association of saintly persons and it is the external manifestation of the seed of the creeper of *bhakti*.

Śrī-nāma-saṅkīrtana–congregational chanting of Śrī Kṛṣṇa's holy names.

Śṛṅgāra-rasa–another name for *mādhurya-rasa*, the mellow of devotion where the devotee's love for Śrī Kṛṣṇa is expressed in the mood of a lover.

Śuddha-bhakti–pure devotion; that is, devotion which is unmixed with fruitive action or monistic knowledge and which is devoid of all desires other than the desire to provide Śrī Kṛṣṇa with pleasure.

Sukṛti–pious activity which, upon sufficient accumulation, can produce faith in transcendental entities such as the words of the scriptures and saintly persons and the process of devotional life.

Svarūpa-śakti–Bhagavān's divine potency is known as *svarūpa-śakti*. It is called *svarūpa-śakti* because it is situated in His own form (*svarūpa*). This potency is fully conscious (*cinmaya*), and thus it is the counterpart and antithesis of matter. Consequently, it is also known as *cit-śakti*, or potency endowed with consciousness. Because this potency is intimately connected with the Lord, being situated in His form, it is further known as *antaraṅga-śakti*, or internal potency. Because it is superior to His marginal and external potencies both in form and glory, it is known as *parā-śakti*, or superior potency. Thus, by its qualities, this potency is known by different names–*svarūpa-śakti*, *cit-śakti*, *antaraṅga-śakti* and *parā-śakti*.

Svarūpa-siddhā-bhakti–all endeavours of the body, words and mind which are related to Śrī Kṛṣṇa and which are performed exclusively and directly for His pleasure without any intervention are known as *svarūpa-siddhā-bhakti*.

T

Tulasī-mālā–a necklace of beads which is composed of wood from the sacred *tulasī* plant. It is worn by all devotees of Śrī Kṛṣṇa.

U

Uttamā-bhakti–the topmost devotion. This is described in *Bhakti-rasāmṛta-sindhu* (1.1.11) as follows: "The cultivation of activities which are meant exclusively for the pleasure of Śrī Kṛṣṇa, or in other words the uninterrupted flow of service to Śrī Kṛṣṇa, performed through all endeavours of the body, mind and speech, and through the expression of various spiritual sentiments (*bhāvas*), which is not covered by knowledge aimed at impersonal liberation (*jñāna*) and reward-seeking activity (*karma*), and which is devoid of all desires other than the aspiration to bring happiness to Śrī Kṛṣṇa, is called *uttamā-bhakti*, pure devotional service."

Uttama* or *mahā-bhāgavata–the topmost devotee, who has attained perfection in his devotion unto Śrī Kṛṣṇa.

V

Vaidhī–devotion which is prompted by the rules and regulations of the scriptures.

Varṇāśrama–the Vedic social system, which organises society into four occupational divisions (*varṇas*) and four stages of life (*āśramas*).

Vātsalya-rasa–one of the five primary relationships with Śrī Kṛṣṇa which is established within the devotee's heart in the perfectional stage of *bhāva* or *prema*. In this relationship, the devotee's love for the Lord is expressed in the mood of parenthood.

Vipralambha–the love that is felt when separated from one's beloved.

Vraja-rasa–the devotional mellows (*rasas*) with which Śrī Kṛṣṇa's eternal devotees serve Him in the eternal abode of Vraja, or Vṛndāvana.

Vraja-parikaras–Śrī Kṛṣṇa's eternal devotees who reside in the transcendental abode of Vraja, or Vṛndāvana.

Vraja-vāsīs–the residents of either the Vṛndāvana situated in the spiritual world (Goloka) or the Vṛndāvana situated within the material realm (Gokula).

Y

Yukta-vairāgya–appropriate renunciation; renunciation which is suitable for entrance into devotional life. This is defined in *Bhakti-rasāmṛta-sindhu* (1.2.255): "When one is detached from material sense enjoyment, but accepts in appropriate proportion objects which are favourable to his devotional practice, and shows special inclination towards things which are directly related to Kṛṣṇa, such as the remnants of foodstuffs which have been offered unto Him, his renunciation is known as *yukta-vairāgya*."

References

Bhagavad-gītā (B-g)
9.30, 31

Bhakti-rasāmṛta-sindhu (B-r-s)
1.2.272, 294, 295

Bhakti-sandarbha (B-s)
236, 868

Caitanya-Bhāgavat (C-B)
One reference

Caitanya-caritāmṛta (C-c)
Madhya-līlā 22.149, 152, 153, 156, 157, 159, 161;
Antya-līlā 6.227, 236, 279

Hari-bhakti-vilāsa (H-b-v)
One reference

Padma Purāṇa (PP)
Four references

Prema-vivarta (P-v)
7.3.1, 2, 3, 4

Śrī Bhaktivinoda Ṭhākura (ŚBṬ)
Three verses

Śrīmad-Bhāgavatam (Ś-B)
3.23.55; 3.25.24; 3.31.34, 39; 7.5.30; 10.2.32, 33; 11.14.24; 11.19.24

Śrī Mukta-caritam (ŚM-c)
Concluding Prayers, 1

Śrī Upadeśāmṛta (ŚU)
1-11

Ujjvala-nīlamaṇi (U-n)
4.5

Verse Index

In the right hand column of this index is found the names of the scriptures from which the verses listed have been cited. The code for the scriptures listed here may be found in the reference table given on pages 131-132.